MACGREGOR'S MIXTURE

MACGREGOR'S MIXTURE

FORBES MACGREGOR

GORDON WRIGHT
55 MARCHMONT ROAD, EDINBURGH, EH9 1HT
SCOTLAND

SBN 903065 15 0

Cover Design and Photograph
by G. Gordon Wright

Printed in Scotland by Lindsay & Co. Ltd., 17 Blackfriars Street
Edinburgh, EH1 1ND

CONTENTS

Forbes Macgregor

Foreword

Scots in general have a reputation for settling old scores, not the best side of their national character. The Macgregors were notorious for taking revenge. Their bloody deeds culminated in the battle of Glen Fruin, near Loch Lomond, in 1603, when they massacred the force that James VI had sent against them. This massacre, and the subsequent harrying of the whole district up to the gates of Glasgow, so shocked the Scots King and parliament that Acts of Proscription were passed aimed at destroying the whole clan, even wiping out the very name. These Acts were not finally lifted until 1787.

In the year 1786 Rob Roy's second son Ranald died at Balquhidder, aged 84. It was the end of an age of violence in the Highlands, and the Macgregors rejoined civilised society, providing distinguished men in all walks of life. Dr James Gregory, head of the Edinburgh Medical School, foremost in the world at that time, was a near relation of Rob Roy. As might be expected, he was a pretty grim fellow, nicknamed "The Starving Doctor", for he was down on Drink and Gluttony. His legacy to suffering humanity was a stomachic medicine, "Dr Gregory's Mixture" so unpleasant that a spoonful of jam had to be kept ready to counteract its taste.

My family being originally Glengyle Macgregors, from the head of Loch Katrine in the Trossachs, we take after Rob Roy in this respect; no matter how grim the circumstances, we like to spice them with humour. I thought that, on attaining my three score and ten, I would use my experience of Scottish life to present a collection of amusing and curious tales to the public. To serve as a "large spoonful of jam" I have concocted "Macgregor's Mixture", which may help to compensate for the miseries of the past.

7

BAIRNS

In practically every respect Scottish bairns are like children all the world over. Children's charm lies in their innocence, and the fresh and frank way they see life and make comments on it. But in at least two respects Scottish 'weans' are unique: they have a long tradition of intellectual pre-eminence to live up to, which gives them a certain gravity of looks and speech; and like their race they tend to be very practical and in this way they often shock more sentimental adults. Scotland abounds with humorous stories about bairns.

I have known the Canongate of Edinburgh and its folk intimately for over fifty years and I can vouch for the truth of these tales.

The infants' mistress in a Canongate school had just informed the children that nobody in the whole world knew where God lived.

"Does he no live in Heaven, miss?" queried one wee lassie.

"Yes, he does, but nobody knows where it is".

"I ken whaur he bides," cried out another, eagerly.

"How can *you* know, when not even the wise people know?"

"Aye, but I do, but. He bides in 192 Canongate, As I cam by tae the schule this moarnin I heard a wumman cry, "Goad, are ye no up yet?"

Another class of infants were asked either to draw Jesus as a boy setting off to Jerusalem to the synagogue, or entering Jerusalem mounted on an ass. As might have been expected, some remarkable drawings were handed in. The boy Jesus was carrying an attache-case with J.C. printed on it. This was reasonable, but

9

one drawing was so curious that the teacher asked the artist for an explanation.

"Please, miss, I couldnae draw a cuddy, so I pit him comin' up the street on a scooter."

In the depression of the "General Strike" era, 1926, lucky bairns had scooters; the majority made "guiders" of soap-boxes and pram wheels, but one very well-off lad boasted a Fairy Cycle (second-hand). In Leith's dockland area the headmaster, a man of classical and biblical erudition, was conferring with his head teacher and janitor, when a breathless urchin rushed in without knocking and cried out, "Please, jany, will ye come oot and speak tae Willie Broon, for he's ridin' my fairy."

After an exchange of mystified glances, and some speculation about this latter-day manifestation of the supernatural in the heart of Leith, the three men realised that the boy meant his Fairy Cycle.

A stout infants' mistress was giving a nature study lesson on birds. She made the Canary the subject of her talk and was pretty certain at the end of ten minutes that her pupils all knew that canaries trill, eat seed, and perch on a spar.

"Now," she summed up, "Who can tell me something a canary does, that I can't do?"

An eager hand shoots up.

"Yes, Freddie."

"Please miss. Tak' a dook in a saucer."

A wee boy was being shown a large coloured Bible picture of "Daniel in the Lions' Den". The prophet is bravely confronting his intending devourers, three large snarling beasts: in the background are others, ready to pounce and in perspective yet another hungry animal.

The lad tearfully pointed his finger at the farthest-off lion. "Thon puir wee lion is hungry tae, and he's no tae be gettin' ony."

The inspector was examining the school on scripture and he did not seem to be aware that he was well over the heads of the bairns. He was expounding the text "Except ye be born again . . . ye shall not enter the Kingdom of Heaven."

"How many of you would like to be born again?"

Every hand shot up but one, a small boy's.

"Come now, laddie, would you not like to be born again so that you might enter the Kingdom of Heaven?"

"Na."

"Why not?"

"Please, sir, I micht be born a lassie."

The devil has many haunts in Scotland but two or three towns are proverbially associated with His Satanic Majesty's residence; Forfar, Ayr, and Kirkcaldy.

A minister had received a call from a quiet country parish to a kirk in the Lang Toon. In the intervals of packing, on the eve of the flitting, he overheard his young daughter saying her bedtime prayers, which ended: "Bless Mummy and Daddy, and good-bye, dear God. I'm going away to Kirkcaldy in the morning."

Small children have in all ages played at building houses with whatever was handy. Very recently, in these days of industrial strife, a few wee bairns were house-building when an elderly passerby asked them what they were doing.

10

"Buildin' hooses."

"But you have stopped. Are you on strike?"

"Naw. We're buggared for bricks."

A minister approached a group playing with a toy lorry and a spade and showed a kindly interest. Addressing the boy pulling the lorry, he asked,

"What are you playing at, sonny?"

"Funerals."

"And whom are you burying?"

"A deid man."

"And what is his name?"

The small boy looked up and snorted.

"Hm. Hoo the hell d'ye think I ken? I'm just the bloody cuddy."

Another reverend gentleman, very portly, stopped to watch a wee lad up to the elbows in mud, by the village duckpond. Some of the shapes looked like houses, others could have been anything, so the minister began to ask what they were.

"It's oor village wi' the kirk an the hooses and the hotel an a' yon wee line o' dottles is the fowk gaun intae the kirk."

"But where's the minister, Tommy? Ye mustna forget the minister."

"O, him," said Tommy, without looking up to see his questioner, "We'll hae to dae withoot him the-day. Ye see there's no eneuch muck left in the hale dub to mak him."

The sins of the fathers and mothers are visited on the children, especially when the fathers and mothers have visitors.

Sir Walter Scott was highly amused by a true tale from the Fair Isle, one of the remotest inhabited isles of Scotland. The minister came very infrequently to perform the religious ceremonies of baptism and marriage. Children were often several years old when baptised.

A boy of between three and four was being baptised. As the minister sprinkled his face, the child found the water a bit chilly and exclaimed "Deil be in you fingers, mun."

Some families are lax at saying grace. One such family with a small boy were having tea with a pious household. When the adults had all closed their eyes to await the longish grace, the young innocent piped out, "Why are they all doing wee sleepies?"

No actor in his senses tries to compete with children and animals. They belong to a different world. Children are much more interested in animals than they are in adult humans, whom they find a pretty dull lot.

A British resident in Khartoum used to take his son down each Saturday to pay homage to Gordon, whose statue, perched high on a dromedary, stands in a prominent position by the river.

Time came for the gentleman to go on leave, so he took his son down to pay a farewell visit to the martyred Briton.

"Now, my son, for the last time, you and I shall salute Gordon. But before you do so, have you any questions you wish to ask?"

"Just one, daddy. Who is the funny man on Gordon's back?"

11

A family who had never been near a city, and were hired to work in a farm near a fashionable city district, sent their son to begin school. The Infant Mistress, a lady of delicate appetites, was persuading him to finish off his first school dinner of a rather 'gusty' stew. He did his best, then laid down his spoon (for he could not handle knives and forks), and looking up at her with a sigh of repletion remarked in the broadest Doric, as he laid his hand on his stomach:

"Ah cannae. I'm fu'. My kyte's fair steched. I doot ye'll hae to eat it yersel." At the very idea she beat a hasty retreat.

Shepherds' bairns are well educated in the ways of sheep before they start school, and some can deliver lambs, so they have little need of lessons on "the birds and the bees."

The inspector called at a school in a pastoral parish. The lady teacher was asked to take a nature lesson. She hung up a large picture of a sheep.

"Now, children, what is that?"

Not a hand went up.

"Oh, come away. Surely you all know what it is?"

Still no response, so in desperation she called on a wee lass.

"Come on, Jenny Scott. You must know. Your dad is a shepherd."

"I'm no richt sure, miss. Jock here says it's a Cheviot gimmer but I think mysel it's a half-bred Leicester cross."

Although many bairns have the attraction of being innocent there are quite a few who have more than their share of original sin, or cheekiness, which has no respect for the niceties of life.

A small boy had a three mile walk to school across a lonely moor. At the first bend of the road near some trees he was out of sight of the house. He crouched down under a bank, opened his school bag, not to look at his books, but to see what fillings were in his sandwiches. Then in a disgusted phrase, which echoed his father's language, he exclaimed to the vast horizon,

"Hm. Cheese again. Ye wad think I was a bloody moose."

In a classroom, somewhere west of Suez and east of Camlachie Toll, the young lady teacher was doing her best to add colour to the dreary semi-ecclesiastic surroundings. She asked the bairns to bring a flower, or a decoration. After the dinner-break to her joy (short-lived) a wee "shilpet" laddie brought an enormous lily. "O, Jim, what a gorgeous flower." Then she had an unworthy second thought. "Where did you get it?"

"I goat it aff the ludger's coaffin, an if he's no buriet the morn I'll bring ye anither yin."

A benevolent old gentleman on a sight-seeing tour in the Old Town of Edinburgh, was accosted by a wee ragamuffin who offered to act as guide for a small fee. The gentleman was much taken with the lad's initiative and intelligence and asked him about his education. He was attending a nearby school, on as few occasions as he could, he confessed. "But," he said proudly, "I have a brother at the University." This touched the springs of generosity and the old man handed him two half-crowns. "That's to help your brother with his studies. What Faculty is he in?"

"O, he's no in a Faculty. He was born wi twa heids and he's in a boattle."

A true tale from Duns, to show the degeneracy of the modern Scots country-man compared with the tough generations who thought no ill of "dichtin' their dowps wi' dockens." A five-year-old lassie pushed her way through the queue and demanded, "I've come for the toilet-roll my mither ordered. An' she said I was to hurry, for faither's sittin' waitin' for it."

The full rigours of education have been tempered nowadays but in the distant past it was a cruel introduction to the fields of intellectual pleasure. There was no royal road to learning either, as King James VI of Scotland soon found out. His tutor was George Buchanan, one of the most scholarly of men, who did not suffer fools gladly, even the "wisest fool in Christendom." The young King pushed his luck too far and George chastised him. James went wailing off and returned with one of the ladies of the court who demanded of Buchanan,
"What have you dared to do to his sacred Majesty's person?"
The grave scholar replied,
"I hae skelpit his arse, Madam. Ye may kiss it an ye please."
It is said that all his life King James had nightmares in which Buchanan played the principal role.

The compulsory Education Act of 1872 was perhaps necessary to correct illiteracy, especially in the cities, but it tended to treat all scholars as conscripts when a large percentage of them were eager volunteers. In any case it was an alien culture that was thrust upon the majority of Scots, as the following stories show.
A wee lass returned sadly after a bad day at school.
"Maw," she complained, "I'm fed up. I wish I hadnae goed to schule."
Maw turned on her.
"Is that hoo they learn ye to speak? What ye mean is, ye wish to Goad ye hadnae went."
Another was being taught to say "Please" and "Thank you" and was told to practise this at home at dinner-time as it would help to sweeten the domestic scene. She returned to afternoon school looking woe-begone.
"Dear me, what's wrong, Sarah?" asked the teacher.
"Please, miss, I done like what ye tellt us, but ma mither just skelpt ma lugs and said, "Ye're hellish polite the day. That'll learn ye not to tak the mickie oot o' me.'"
A lass of tender years, put in the dunce's corner, was heard muttering. The teacher at last heard what she was saying.
"I wish I was marriet and awa oot o' this," a sentiment with which the young school-marm heartily agreed.
Marriage has always been a Promised Land, and as the next chapter will illustrate, this promise has been fulfilled in varying degrees. A young pupil was asked to write a short essay on what she would do if she were a housewife.
"I would get my man and bairns their porridge and then I would get them to school. Then I would synd out the plates and do out the budgie's cage. Then I would go and have a good hing ower the windae."

One teacher rather daringly asked the class how mother set about having a baby. She was informed to her surprise.
"She washes her feet, puts on her best nightie, gets into bed and sends for granny."

It is a good principle in education not to warn children about any temptations they have never heard of, and cannot understand. There is little point in warning young children about alcoholism, or promiscuous sex, for they see the world through their own eyes.

A teacher asked her class to name the members of their family. Most answers were normal, but one lass puzzled the teacher.

"There's Jeannie and wee Tam; there's Ma (Faither's deid) and the goldfish and Feardie."

"Is Feardie the dog?"

"Na, we've nae dug. Feardie's the ludger."

"That's a funny name."

"It's his nickname. He's feared to sleep himsel. He has to sleep wi' Ma."

The Scots were a thrifty people and rarely failed to turn old material into new articles, though they did not like friends and neighbours to recognise it.

At a tea-party, where a tempting cake was displayed, the son was given a piece, but asked for more. He was refused, and sulked.

"If ye dinna gie me anither bit I'll tell thon."

Still his mother refused, but wondered what 'thon' could be. Her friends pricked up their ears, expecting a juicy domestic morsel. Still the wretch persisted and mother refused. At last she said, "There's nae mair for ye. Ye can tell them if ye like." She was somewhat relieved when he blurted out:

"Ma new breeks are made oot o' the auld parlour curtains."

There is a tale about young Robert Burns and his brother Gilbert, which has been vouched for as true, and shows that "as the twig's inclined, the tree will grow." (Gilbert by the way when a boy, was considered much the mental superior of his brother.) The pair were seen digging a hole and were asked what it was for. Robert replied roguishly, "It's to bury Auld Nick." "How are you going to catch him?" Robert burst into peals of laughter. "Aye, that's the bit. Hoo are we gaun to catch the auld rascal?"

Scotland was keen on theology, so the scholars were well drilled in it. They had to learn 107 questions and answers in the Shorter Catechism, all of which were quite beyond them. These, as I remember with disgust, were in a thin booklet in brick-red covers, with the arms of Glasgow on the front. When catechisms were later printed in Falkirk they were regarded with superstitious horror because they did not have "The bell that never rang, the fish that never swam, the bird that never flew, the tree that never grew." This booklet with the multiplication tables on the back cost a halfpenny.

It sounds incredible, but it was known for the teacher to demand an answer to the "umbrella" question, "What does God do to me?" and take the tawse to those who couldn't supply the answer, which, according to him was, "God loves me."

"Who killed Cain?" was put to a small boy, in an aggressive tone, and got the trembling answer, "Please, sir, it wasnae me."

LOVE

This is a very broad field to be turned loose in, and there are many bye-laws to confuse or guide, as the case may be. The oldest is "To err is human, to love divine," which is rather vague.

There are probably more taboos about love or sex than about any other human business, in every community civilised or primitive, though the latter are usually more strict.

Scotland, even when the Romans came, had very mixed populations. The Romans brought troops from Europe, Africa and Asia, and since then it has been mixed even more, so we can expect all kinds of sex behaviour, leading to amusing, even scandalous tales.

For a long time, as readers of Victorian literature know, there was a normal love-life. Boy met girl etc. and it finished up, perhaps, with a 'golden' photo in the local press.

There seemed to be no room for humour in this even course of love, but sometimes there was. First, in courtship: Scots were reputed to be canny: none of the dashing Latin temperament, the bottom-pinching or the Gallic fire, the Don Juan or Casanova. Well, girls shouldn't always bank on this, but courtship was seldom impulsive.

A wealthy Lothians farmer about thirty, had a pretty girl in mind so he popped the question and was accepted. He then explained that he was very busy with the farm management.

"I can weel understand," said the lady, "but I'll hae ye, and mak nae banes aboot it. But mind this, when the tatty-plantin' is ower, and the neeps sawn, I maun hae my dues o' the coortin'."

There have been mean lovers. One such miser took his lady-love to Edinburgh for a day's outing. She paid her own fare. He dragged her round all the many free places of entertainment till she was ready to drop, and never offered even a cup of tea. At last, as they awaited the train for home, a generous feeling came over

15

him. He put two pennies into the chocolate machine and handed her one of the meagre bars.

When she got home, she poured out her woeful tale to her mother, who burst out in wrath, "Gang richt doon noo to his hoose and gie him back his penny. That'll affront him." The lassie did as bidden and handed him the penny. "Och," said he, "There wisnae sic a hurry. It wad hae done on Monday."

A wooing often dragged on from year to year: as some sarcastic folk said, "They were waiting for the minister to grow up." But a canny Fife couple "had had an understanding" for nearly thirty years. At last, on a balmy summer evening, the lunatic influence of the full moon stirred the lady to unmaidenly action.

"Freddie," she breathed, "Is it no aboot time we were gettin' mairret?" A heavy silence, then Freddie sighed, "Aye, Elspeth, it is that." A hopeful gleam came into her eye. "Aye, fully time, lass. But wha wad hae us?"

A pretty girl found safety in numbers, as often as in exodus. A saucy young belle, realising that there was competition for her company, made the most of it. It came as a great shock to one of her followers to realise that she was flirting furiously with several others. He confronted her angrily, "I'm not going to play second fiddle to anyone," he announced. She retorted coolly. "H'm, play second fiddle. With an instrument like yours, you're damned lucky to be in the band at a'."

A douce-living Border lady had been told by her doctor that at fourscore she could not expect to see the winter out. She went round to pay her outstanding bills, and called on the joiner and undertaker.

"I'll dae my best for ye, Miss Trummle, as ye ken, but what kind o' a lining will ye want? It's purple for the mairret leddies and white for the unmairret."

"Weel, Bob, I'll hae to hae white, I suppose, but wad ye steek on twa-three purple swatches just to show I've no been a'thegither negleckit."

Courting was a difficult business for there were few sheltered places where this could be carried on. There were, in some areas, not even small thickets like that wood in Northumberland known as "Ha'penny Wood" at Framlington which was hired out to couples for that fee. However, a very wide stocking was knitted in the northern isles, which admitted an amorous couple but forbade intercourse. In this they were bedded for a twenty-hour night of modified ecstasy.

Sir Walter Scott's direct ancestor was Scott of Harden. His handsome son was caught lifting cattle and was taken to the gallows-hill and a noose put round his neck. Then he was given an option: either be hanged, or marry any woman who would save him from his fate. The prosecutor had a very plain (homely) daughter known locally as "Muckle Moo'ed Meg" named after the famous 15th century cannon, Mons Meg. After one look at Meg the condemned man chose the noose, but changed his mind on a moment's reflection, and married the lady. Theirs was a fruitful union, despite her looks.

Whether folk married or not, some of them regretted it. During the Boer War one old lady in the North was asked to help in a campaign to recruit men for a

16

new regiment. Indignantly she replied, "Na, na, nae fear. I was ne'er able to raise a man for masel. I'm no fashin' to raise yin for Queen Victoria."

At a fine summer wedding in Glasgow the confetti was flying and the happy pair were accompanied by cheers, ribbons, old boots and "poor-oots". But an old maiden lady onlooker did not enter into the spirit of the occasion at all.
"Solemn events, marriages and deaths," she muttered, shaking her head.
An old married lady, a former rival, clapped her on the shoulder saying, "Eh, Phemie, ye've been lang spared."

Shyness has long led to celibacy and this is likely to apply to males as well as females. A border lady had never married, and as she was known to have a tidy bank account and was pretty, it remained a mystery for many years how she was allowed to sustain the burden of her virginity. However, at the railway junction at St. Boswells, the stationmaster discovered her secret fear by chance. She had lost her trunk and ran up and down "fair dementit", until it was traced to the guard's van.
"Eh, it's a Lord's mercy," she exclaimed, relieved, "I'm prepared for ony pairtins we may be ca'ed upon to mak in this vale o' tears, but I ne'er could stand the thocht o' pairtin' frae my claes."

In the Highlands, especially in Upper Strathspey, it was not considered immoral for a man and a woman to live together unmarried for a year. If a child was born, some arrangement for its welfare was made, the mother usually keeping it. She was known as a grace or grass widow, a term nowadays often applied to women whose husbands play a lot of golf.

Girls do not always disclose how they were seduced, and if they do, it is not often in such telling phrases as the Newhaven lassie's, last century, during the era of the Sankey and Moody revival meetings. For sheer artistry in words, happily married to feelings, I think this true account, told me by a reliable witness, takes a lot of beating.
"Last Setterday nicht efter the Gospel meetin' Jamie Carnie took me to the Halley, wheecht aff my ham-cloots, and cowpt me doon on the gress. He lowsed his cowp-cairt. The neist thing I kent something gaed up my rig-bane like a flicht o' swallies and I met the blessed angels."

An old man, very ill, was rather cruelly asked by the Calvinistic "Auld Licht" minister, "Are ye no afraid to meet the King of Terrors?"
"No me," he replied, "I was mairret to his sister for thirty years."

At a golden wedding the old bridegroom was laying off to the bored party at the dinner about his long and happy marriage, and about the good guidance the Holy Bible had been to him. But his sanctimonious recommendations fell short of their intended effect when the auld wife interrupted in a stage whisper,
"Sit ye doon, ye auld whited sepulchre; gin ye had lifted the brods o' the faimily Bible as aften as ye lifted up the skirts o' my nicht-goon, ye'd hae been a muckle better man the day."

A younger, but still a pious, bridegroom in the land of the Westland Whigs, not a mile from Cumnock, knelt an extravagantly long time at the bedside where his bride patiently waited.

"Whit ails ye, Dauvit, dinna say ye're sweir to bed?"

"Na, I'm praying to the Lord for strength and guidance."

"Lowp in under the claes then. You provide the strength and I'll gie ye the guidance."

A kindly but inquisitive old lady in the Borders, who lived for other people (who could be distinguished by their hunted looks), made a point of calling whenever a birth had been announced. She visited a cottage in a farm "raw" to see the latest arrival in a family which already numbered a dozen.

Laying down a gift, she asked the mother, "Another olive branch. What is it this time?"

"A lassie."

"Dearie me, It was a lassie last time. Is it aye a lassie?"

"Naw, thank God, thoosands o' times naething ava."

Burns acquired a traditional reputation for love-making, which cannot be fully justified. Many stories of his sexual prowess still continue to circulate in Scotland, but it is to be feared that most of them are unjustly fathered on him.

The tale goes that, as Rabbie was crossing the Meadows in Edinburgh, he met a woman carrying a basket of eggs. She said, "Are you the famous poet Rabbie Burns?" "That I am, my dear lass, at your service." "O, if that's the wey o't," she replied in a resigned tone, "I suppose I'll hae to pit doon my basket o' eggs."

Burns was said to be carrying a lusty young pig under his arm on a quiet hill road, when he met a woman coming down from the common with an empty clothes basket. She mounted the road-side bank to avoid him.

"What's ailing you, wumman? Are ye feard for me?"

"Aye, I thocht ye were gaun to set tae me."

"Hoo the deil could I set tae ye, wumman, when it taks me a' ma time to haud this grice?"

"O, I thocht ye wad pit the beast under my basket, and pit a stane on tap o't."

In 1897, the year of Queen Victoria's diamond Jubilee, two ladies were arguing about the meaning of the word. They decided to consult a third party, another lady like themselves who had been married for some years. She explained.

"Weel, ye see, it's like this. When ye've been mairret for five and twenty years that's your Silver. When ye've been mairret for fifty years that's your Gowden. And when your man dees, that's your Jubilee."

The farmer saw a suspicious glow in his barn and hurried to investigate. He found a young lad with a lantern.

"What are ye daein' here wi' a lantern aroond my coorts?"

"I'm coortin' your lassie and it's a gey dark nicht."

"I ne'er heard the like o't. When I was a young lad I ne'er cairried a lantern to gang coortin' ma lass."

"I can understand that," said the lad. "I've seen your wife."

The new-married wife was of a thrifty nature and she made a bargain with her husband that every time he kissed her he would put a bawbee in the piggy-bank. A penny would mark a more uxorious embrace. At the end of six months the

18

piggy-bank was full so they decided to break it open. To the husband's joy and surprise a large number of sixpences and shillings rolled out among the coppers. He questioned her so suspiciously that she sharply got in the candid explanation. "Weel, it means that folk are no' a' sae economical as you."

Country folk would have a pretty thin time were it not for God's ordinance of sex, for how could there be an increase in the flocks and herds without it, (barring artificial insemination.)

A handsome widow-woman had been granted a cottage and a bit of land not far from the farm where her husband had worked. She earned a little by doing odd chores, and kept a few fowls, a cow and a pig as well as a garden. One fine morning the farmer called in on passing and asked her how she was getting on.

She answered in all innocence, "Brawly, thank you. My coo's bulled and my soo's brant and I'm in grand fettle mysel."

There was little time for the aesthetic in many outlying parts. Life was harsh and a living was "ill to win." A hard-working farmer, well on in years, called on the minister and confided that at last he had some thoughts about marriage, as he had gathered a tidy bit of gear.

"Do you realise, Willie, all that marriage entails?"

Willie nodded.

"I don't think you fully realise the holiness of the sacrament."

The good man explained about the banns, the ceremony, the responses, the ring.

Willie made for the door.

"I'm glad you have decided to consider it well, Willie."

Willie turned.

"I hae that, meenister, and I think, a' things considered, I'll just hure it oot."

Aberlady, East Lothian, had a reputation for ladies of pleasure. James IV kept three mistresses here, whose names were Sandilands, Weir and Oliphant. Sir David Lindsay, the satirist, author of "The Thrie Estates", had a good deal of licence in court and openly admonished the King in the punning verse.

"Sow not your seed on sandy lands
Waste not your strength in weir (weariness or restriction)
And ride not on an oliphant (elephant)
For spoiling of your gear."

An Aberlady husband caught his wife in the act and flew into a rage. He chased the guilty pair up the street, brandishing his dagger. On being asked by a few women what was the cause of his rage, he told them, but got the following cool reply,

"Is that a'; then stick us a' in Aberlady." Any stranger, who wanted to start a riot in later, more decorous, ages, had simply to shout the proverbial "Stick us a' in Aberlady."

At weddings in Edinburgh this card was often attached to the bridal coach, "Aberlady tonight, Kenmore tomorrow."

The scene shifts to a lonely parish in grassy Argyll where the Free Kirk Session of Achaglachlach were met.

Said the minister, "Noo, my friends, I'm preventit this year frae attending the Assembly in Embro, sae yin o' ye will hae to deputise for me. But I maun hae a

19

venerable and God-fearing elder to go. I think auld Archie MacCorquodale is oor man. He's fower-score, and no likely to be enticed by the allurements o' Vanity Fair."

So old MacCorquodale set off for the two weeks, but it was a month before he returned. The session was convened.

"Noo, Archie, this lang absence in the Babylon o' the Lothians calls for an explanation."

"Weel, minister, there was the Assembly for a hale week and then anither week o' the committees."

"Aye, that's half the time."

"Weel, there was a wee bit sociality."

"Nae doot," said the minister drily," and whisky,—and weemin."

"I'll no deny whisky looks gey weel on the table."

Finally the inquisition got old MacCorquodale to his knees in penitence.

"Oh, sir, ye wad forgie me a' my transgressions, gin ye kent what it was to lie in the experienced airms o' an abandoned wumman, efter five and fifty years o' humdrum cohabitation wi Mrs MacCorquodale."

All these tales show the broad-minded attitude of the Scot towards love. This could perhaps be best rounded off by a Scottish version of the world's first love story, Adam and Eve. According to the Jewish Talmud the whole story took only twelve hours.

Twal Oors in Paradise

The Lord's taen up twal stane o' stour
To mak a man within the oor;
He filled it neist wi bluid and sweit
And stude the cratur on its feet:
"For twa oors noo gie nomenclature
To a' the bestiary o' natur!"
Then God gied him an oor's sedation,
Cut oot his rib for Eve's creation;
When he awoke the simple eediot
Fell deep in love and wed immediate;
For three oors withoot kirk or papers
They cut some matrimonial capers,
Tho' Eve foond time twixt copulations
To share wi Satan fruit collations;
Wi Knowledge o' the guid and evil
She glaikt puir Adam to the Deevil;
And or the nock had chappit twice
God pit them oot o' Paradise.

MEAT & MUSIC

"There's baith meat and music here," said the dog when he ate the bag-pipes. He could make no attempt to compose a pibroch, or a serious and elaborate piece such as "The Birlinn of Clan Ranald." Neither can I. Any music I refer to is purely incidental.

The earliest inhabitants of "Scotland" who lived in underground houses such as Maes Howe, in Orkney, ate fish, flesh and grain, as remains show. Animals were plentiful and whales frequently stranded themselves as they still do, providing rather too much meat, but enough oil for years of lighting and cooking.

Whale meat is not to our modern taste. During the last war it was eaten, like dried eggs, without enthusiasm, except in one instance, when a customer in a restaurant ordered a second helping, and a third, to the gratification and amazement of the restaurateur. "I trust you will favour us with your custom regularly, sir. We shall be delighted to reserve lunch for you each day. Do you prefer whale-meat?"

"Indeed I do."

"May I make a note of your name?"

"Certainly, my name is Jonah, and I've waited a long time for this."

A delicate lady of genteel tastes was invited to a farm. The table was piled with delicacies, boiled ham, tongue, scones, jam. The farmer sliced at the ox tongue and piled it on to her plate. She smiled wanly and simpered, "No, thank ye, I

21

couldn't eat onything that has come oot o' a beast's mooth."

Her host thought for a minute or two, then suggested, "Maybe ye'd raither hae a biled egg, then?"

Not nearly so delicate was an old lady who went around complaining about her failing digestive powers. Her motto seems to have been, "Better belly burst than guid meat wasted." One of her grumbles was this: "I dinna ken what's come ower me these days. I canna eat a bitty biled ham twice the buik o' ma steikit neive but I hae the ruft o't the hale efternin." At today's prices two pounds of ham would be prohibitive.

A holiday-maker in the north was being given fish at every meal so he sent to Edinburgh for a box of sausages. He gave them to the landlady to prepare them for his breakfast. He was dismayed next morning to see fried sausage skins on his plate. On asking an explanation he was told, "Weel, that was all that was left of them, after I had gutted them."

Bad cooks are nobody's friends. The famous hanging judge Lord Braxfield, on whose character Stevenson formed Weir of Hermiston, was a man who could not tolerate bad cooking. A lassie was recommended to him as a cook in these words,

"She's a very decent young woman."

"Damn her decency," he cried, "Can she mak' guid collops?" (mince.)

He got no assurance on this point so he went on,

"Gie me a lassie that can plain-bile a tattie even if she was but a hure aff the streets."

Plain-boiling of potatoes was one of the tests of a good cook, it seems, for by Braxfield's time, about 1790, potatoes were plentiful. Their cultivation was easy, compared with peas, beans and grain, though many people condemned them. A very pompous person was trying to impress some of the inhabitants of a Border town (which had had the honour of giving him birth), just how well he had prospered in the Army (in the catering department).

He gave out that he was of high rank in the 'Commissariat,' and he asked an old wifie if she knew the meaning of the word. She quickly deflated his ego.

"I ken this muckle, for as stupid as ye think I am, it has something to dae wi' the dreepin' o' the tatties."

When English persons of gentility wished to use a polite expression for going to the toilet they were "watering their roses." In the Scottish rural areas they were awa' to "dreep their tatties."

As in the present world set-up, when whole nations are famine-stricken while others are gluttonous, so it was in old Scotland during the distressed decades which ushered in the 19th century. Weavers, who constituted a large proportion of the working population, were quite prosperous around 1790, but as reliable figures show, their earnings dropped steadily until in the Hungry Forties they were on starvation level. In 1820 there were strikes and severely repressive measures in Glasgow and district, owing to lack of food chiefly. Yet there were those in that city who lived in the greatest indulgence, as this tale of truth (published at that time) shows.

Professor James Gregory (of the Mixture fame) interviewed a prosperous

22

Glasgow merchant who had come through specially to see the "Starving Doctor" about his health.

Dr Gregory ... Good morning, sir. I hear your health is causing you some concern?

Merchant ... Indeed it is. But you must understand I'm one of the plainest living men in the west country.

Dr G. ... Do you take breakfast, sir?

Merchant ... Weel, no what you would ca' breakfast. Just a rizzert haddock, and twa poached eggs, and an oatcake or twa, wi marmalade.

Dr G. ... Do you drink with this?

Merchant ... O, very little. A cup or two of tea, and maybe a waucht o' porter.

Dr G. ... Do you dine early?

Merchant ... No afore eleeven o'clock.

After a long interrogation, it turns out that the patient has four or five substantial meals a day with snacks between times.

Dr G. ... You take supper I suppose?

Merchant ... No sir, I canna be said to take supper. Just something before going to bed. The lug o' a haddie, or a bit toasted cheese, or half a hundred oysters, or the like o' that; two-thirds of a bottle of ale and a tumbler of warm whisky toddy. But I take no regular supper. Only twice a week when I go out do I take a regular supper.

Dr G. ... (severely, when offered a fee.)

No, sir, put up your money. You are a most voracious glutton and drunkard, and unless you reform you have about half a year to live.

Exit the Glesca glutton, a bit puzzled and peeved.

At the time of this interview there were so many distressed areas all over Britain and in Ireland (where this forewarning of the terrible potato famine went unheeded) that relief work had to be provided in the shape of the "Radical Road" in the Royal Park of Holyrood and the "Destitution Road" about Little Loch Broom near Ullapool. James Wilson, a weaver, was forced to go to America because of his political views. He, in association with the artist Anderson, created the classical "Birds of America", now priceless. But in Scotland he suffered extreme poverty and wrote a serio-comic song on this called "Auld Auchtertool," where he relates his experiences in trying to get food and lodging in this Fife village.

"Gin ye gang there for lodgings ye're surely a fool
There's nocht but starvation in auld Auchtertool."

Starvation is a much abused word in English and often means no more than a bit of fasting, but actually means to die. And this is what happened in lowland Scotland in times of bad harvests. The Highlanders were tougher, as we know, and could get along on very little. The proverb says "Ye can aye get a drink oot o' the burn when ye canna get a bite aff the brae." When the clans marched with Charlie they often mixed a little meal and water in their brogues and lived on nothing else. Up till fairly modern times crofters prepared a large pot of porridge or brose. This was often poured into a drawer, left to solidify and cut out in squares, to be heated and supped as required.

Haggis was a sumptuous repast for many, Now it is mainly a symbol of the past and of Burnsian tradition, though many enjoy it. Although the serio-comic "Address" runs down French and Italian foods, this was Burns going all

23

patriotic in the middle of a war against most of Europe. He had momentarily decided to forget that the French "hachis" is just a form of haggis.

The wiles of the poaching trade are many and varied when it comes to catching fish. One of the traditional sports in the three Border counties of Selkirk, Berwick and Roxburgh, from time immemorial was gumping or guddling burn trout or "yella-bellies." The rivers were left to fishermen as their right: they were too wide and deep for the guddlers, whose territory was the small burn usually unfishable because of overhanging bushes and banks.

At Abbey St. Bathan's, deep in the Lammermoor, the landlady of a small inn was sometimes out of provisions when one or two gentlemen, on a fishing trip to the nearby Whitadder, called to put up for the nicht. She would kilt her skirts, take off her shoes and stockings, and guddle the Weir Burn which ran past her house, never failing to catch a panful of sweet burn trout, which she served, fried with oatmeal, and accompanied with eggs and bacon. She never divulged how she caught them.

This little saying, was meant to encourage bairns to eat.

"Tak up your meat, your meat will mak ye bonnie,
And when you're bonny you'll be weel-lo'ed,
And when you're weel lo'ed you'll be licht-herted,
And when you're licht-herted you'll lowp far."

Bannocks is a name to conjure with in Scotland, especially since Bannockburn in 1314. A well-known song is "Bannocks o' barley." A bannock of barley is a very substantial item; it cannot be leavened to any extent and makes a solid meal. There is a wry proverb about bannocks which seems to date from pre-Reformation times for it refers to Friday fasting.

"A bannock is a guid beast; ye may eat its guts on a Friday."

A rather rosy-rustic story is told about bannocks which would put some delicate people off them, if they were still for sale.

A tramp appeared at the back door of a farm carrying what seemed like a large bannock, but was, on closer inspection, a large dry "coo-platt". He asked the farmer's wife if she could spread some butter or jam on it, as he was famished. She went ben the hoose to tell her husband of the poor man's plight. But the farmer knew all about this old rogue and his tricks. He came through to the back-door.

"Eh, ye puir auld hungry soul. This is an awfu' state to be driven to. Throw that cauld yin awa and I'll gie ye a het yin frae the byre."

The Bannock o' Tollishill tells of a more acceptable offering. The tale is quite well-known. Up the Kelphope Burn above Carfraemill in Lauderdale there was a farm named Midside, the ruins of which were still to be seen fifty years ago near the farm of Tollishill. Here lived Midside Maggie.

She went to pay her rent at Thirlestone Castle, or rather to ask for more time to pay, as she had suffered some set-backs. The Duke of Lauderdale's factor was a hard man and told her mockingly that if she brought him a snowball at mid-summer she would live rent-free all her life at Midside. But Maggie was on her mettle. She gathered a huge snowball and buried it covered with heather and turf in a crevice facing north, high up on the Lammermuirs. When Midsummer Eve came she filled a large basket with snow, well happed in wool and straw, and set off the five miles to Lauder.

To the extreme annoyance of the factor she dumped a big snowball on his table and asked him to make good his word. He tried to get out of it but Maggie called for the Duke himself, who kept the pledge. She went rent-free from then on.

Years went by, and the Duke was imprisoned in the Tower of London for his persecutions of the Whigs. Maggie baked a large bannock, but, in lieu of raisins, she stuffed it full of golden guineas. She went by coach to London and gave it to the Duke to alleviate his distress. From this true tale arose the saying: "There was never a bannock like the bannock o' Tollishill."

The grossest act of treachery in Scotland would be hard to decide upon; but surely the betrayal of Wallace by his bosom-friend Graham of Menteith is high on the list. Graham, by the way, was on Bruce's side at Bannockburn, which shows how intricate Scottish mediaeval history is.

However, Scotland did not easily forget the fate of her martyred hero and whenever a Graham of Menteith was entertained to a meal, for centuries after, the bannock was always served to him face down. The proverb remains, "The back o' a bannock to a Menteith", to prove how well this treachery is remembered.

Ham and eggs, like strawberries and cream and other natural partners, was a universally approved dish, but not everyone could afford them. A young wife, who had married a wealthy old dotard, was given the proverbial advice, "Rot him awa wi ham and eggs." With country bairns porridge was the ordinary fare, and to speak of subsisting on ham and eggs was regarded as social snobbery. In a Berwickshire farm row of several workers' houses, the proud mother was given to shouting to her boy to "come and get his ham and eggs," so that all the neighbours would be jealous. However the wind was taken out of her sails one morning when Wee Willie replied, "Pit them doon on the doorstep to cool a bit."

I have not come across the following tale in my readings of Dr Johnson's visit to Scotland with Boswell, but I was told it for gospel, by a truthful man, over fifty years ago.

Johnson and Boswell, in traversing a wide bleak moor, became very hungry. At a modest inn by the wayside, they asked if the lady could provide them with a dinner. She said there was no meat in the house, but Boswell, pointing to the hens scraping about, said she would be well paid if she roasted one for dinner. She consented.

While the meal was being prepared Johnson went for a stroll, while Boswell sat by the fire writing up his diary. The landlady's son, who was turning the spit before the fire, was continually scratching his head. Boswell, knowing too well the primitive hygiene of the country, drew his own conclusions, and when the fowl came to table he would have none of it. Johnson polished the very bones and was so satisfied that, when a large pudding was set down on the table, he could not touch it. However, Boswell, now very hungry, ate it all.

As they were leaving, they paid for their meal and Johnson gave the kitchen boy sixpence, patting him on the head. Boswell also gave him sixpence but did not touch his head. However, he asked him in broad Scots,

"Where's your coul, laddie?" meaning his knitted cap.

"Ma coulie, sir?" piped the lad innocently, "Ma mither biled the pudden in it."

25

There are numerous poetical references to barley, the merriest and most elevating being Burns' "Rigs o' Barley", wherein he describes his amour with Annie Rankine, of which, by the way, her father heartily approved.

One could discourse for hours on Scotland's food, but this is not the place for such details. Books like Marian McNeill's are mines of precious material for gourmets and "plainest-living men" alike.

Many years ago, a stout farmer in Edinburgh was seen running along with a host of small boys in the rear of a horse-drawn fire-engine, furiously proceeding to a fire. The farmer soon ran out of steam and paused, putting some coppers back into his pocket with the remark, "Weel then, ye can keep your damned tatty-chips." The horse-drawn "chippie" was a common sight in city streets then, and with the brass furnishings and smoke it rather resembled a fire-engine.

The local joiner and undertaker paid out the wages on Friday night, and informed his assistant that business was so slack, it being summer, that he would have to pay him off at the end of the following week.

The boy pleaded, "I'll tell ye what, maister, if ye gie me half-wages I'll bide wi' ye for anither three weeks till they begin liftin' the early tatties."

"Licht suppers mak lang days" but great plates of early potatoes, eaten late, were deadly.

Very large helpings of all sorts of food were often served at banquets, and a tale is told of a guest who laid down his knife and fork for a moment and nearly had his plate whisked away by the serving maid.

"Haud on," he cried, "No' sae fast. I've just seen a doo (pigeon) in the redd o' the plate." (i.e. the refuse.)

In the old days folk were fond of their meat, and were blissfully ignorant of protein and vitamin. A country doctor discussed with his patient's wife what kind of meals he was having. It turned out he lived mainly on porridge, scones, potatoes and vegetables. The doctor suggested that he would improve markedly if he had a diet of animal food, meaning beef, mutton or fowl.

A fortnight later the doctor called to see how he was getting on.

"No vera weel," his wife reported, "He manages no sae bad wi the neeps, an the linseed cake. But o, he has a gey sair wrastlin' wi the strae."

The story is told of the farmer at the tenants' dinner, where the gentry mingled, with difficulty, with the locals. A very refined lady asked her home-spun neighbour if he would care for some stewed rhubarb as dessert, to which he replied, "Na, thank ye a' the same, but I dinna need it."

A young Edinburgh medico on the lookout for a practice set off to Musselburgh but was back in Edinburgh in the afternoon. When asked if he had been successful, he replied, "I'm quite satisfied that they have little need for me there. They have large fields of leeks all round the town."

Scotland was the "Land o' Cakes," and when sugar refining became established in the Clyde area, the cake-makers excelled themselves. Nowhere did their art show better than in the "High Tea" beloved of Glasgow and all the big cities. Ham and eggs, and a dozen temptations for hungry football fans, were followed by tiers of cakes.

26

During the '14-18' war a couple of Glasgow kilties with their girl-friends took a table in the most sumptuous of Glasgow's tea-rooms. They had a marvellous meal; the band played patriotic airs and many hero-worshippers smiled at the boys home on leave.

Stern reality had to be faced. Sandy looked at his pal. "Will *you* pey? I'll square up ramorra." "I havenae a bean," confessed Tam. "Whit'll we dae?" Sandy decided to see the manager.

"Are you the manager?"

"I am."

"Weel, whit wad ye dae, if a couppla fellas that've been oot yonder fechtin for the likes o' you, cam in and had a slap-up tea and couldna pay for it?"

The manager lifted a heavy boot.

"D'ye see that boot?"

"Aye, fine that."

"Well, I would give them a hefty kick up the arse for their impudence."

The tough sodger turned about, threw up his kilt, exposed a very sinewy posterior and with the air of one flinging down a five-pound note, exclaimed: "Tak fower high-teas affa that."

Music is a name loosely applied to all kinds of sound. Mary Queen of Scots, on taking up residence at Holyroodhouse, was entertained by an orchestra in the forecourt which nearly drove her out of her mind with its discords and cacophonies. The road to Pandemonium was no doubt paved with good intentions; but Mary had enjoyed better harmonies in the French court, and heartily wished herself back many a time.

She probably also heard Highland music played on the great pipes. But in Europe under the name doedel-zacs (Dutch) or cornemeuse (French) she must have been familiar with some form of pipe-music, which would make her more appreciative of it than many Lowlanders appear to have been.

William Dunbar, in "The Daunce" (of the Seiven Deidly Sins) concludes by bringing a scathing description of Highland bag-piping, which ends thus,

"and in the deepest pot of Hell
He smoorit them with smoke."

There is a tale of a bag-pipe enthusiast who described one of his most delightful experiences in these words:

"Eh, mon, ye should hae been wi' us last Setterday nicht. There was ten o' us a' pipin' awa in Sandy MacPherson's wee back parlour. Mon, it was fair Heevin!" Willie Dunbar would not have agreed.

A keen piper was asked what was the purpose of the drone in the bagpipes, which to a Southern ear was a most distressing sound. He explained it as best he could to the layman, "Weel, ye see, sir, it's chust like this. Withoot the drones we micht as weel be playing the pianny."

At a Highland Games held in Edinburgh a fine pipe band was providing a wonderful background which sent all the Scots blood racing quicker. An Englishwoman turned to me (I wore my Red Macgregor kilt) and said disparagingly "That's not nearly so good as *our* music." "What is *your* music?" I asked. "Oh, the classical music of Beethoven, Handel, Bach and Strauss," she recited, proudly.

27

There is a famous Scottish air called "Whistle ower the Lave o't" which Burns used, though the tune was already old by that time. There is a grimly humorous incident connected with it.

A Glasgow man saw a neighbour, newly buried, rise from his grave, in the precincts of Glasgow Cathedral, and dance a jig with the devil, who played on the pipes the accompanying air, "Whistle ower the Lave o't." The Glasgow magistrates were so aghast at this report that they sent the Town Drummer round the town to forbid anyone either to whistle or play it, on heaviest penalty.

The bells in the steeple of St John's Church in Perth used to play lively Scottish airs every hour. One Sunday at noon the minister had just announced the text "Plough up the fallow ground of your hearts" when the bells began to play "Corn rigs are bonnie," to the great amusement of the whole congregation.

Last century, the precentor at a Highland church was a key man in every sense, for if his tuning fork gave him the wrong key, the whole congregation were at sixes and sevens. No musical instruments were permitted; no organs, which were contemptuously called "kists o' whistles." One Sunday the precentor lost his pitch-fork and asked the carrier to bring him a new one from Perth. The carrier unfortunately knew more about agriculture than music, and handed the precentor a ten-foot pitch-fork "to take up the psalms", with the remark, "You should hae nae trouble roosin' them up to sing wi' this."

Repeating tunes are all very well in secular meetings, but in church they give rise to indecent hilarity.

In the Hundredth Psalm the line "And for his sheep he doth us take" sounded very irreverent when sung as,
"And for his sheep he'd
And for his sheep he'd
And for his sheep he'doth us take."
So did these invocations, when male voices pleaded,
O, send down Sal
O, send down Sal
O, send down Sal-va-tion to us.
and female voices cried,
O, for a man
O, for a man
O for a man-sion in the skies.

The wee lassie was not to be blamed for calling her teddy-bear "Gladly" for there it was in the hymn-book: "Gladly my little cross I'd bear."

The words of hymns and psalms now and then by chance aptly fitted the occasion. In high Victorian times there was a school of religion known humorously as "Muscular Christianity" initiated by Charles Kingsley. Disciples of this sept went in for cold dips, dumb-bells and other scourgings of the flesh.

A young Edinburgh minister, an enthusiastic muscle-man, was appointed as supply-preacher to Dunbar, to which he planned to travel by the early morning express each Sabbath. But on the first Sunday he delayed so long over his keep-fit exercises that he reached the Waverley Station in time to see the rear of the train disappearing into the Calton Tunnel. A porter told him the next train didn't leave till noon, so he resolved to walk. After all, it was a fine fresh summer morning, and the distance 28 miles, was just a little longer than a marathon. However, after Haddington, the heat became excessive; still he struggled on manfully across the dusty plain and reached Dunbar Kirk only half-an-hour late. The precentor had set the congregation on to the 119th psalm, a marathon in itself of 176 verses. They were just starting psalm 62 when the preacher staggered in, to hear this appropriate verse,

"Like as the hart for waterbrooks
In thirst doth pant and bray
So pants my longing soul O God
that come to thee I may."

Psalmody formed an important part of church services amongst the Moderates, but such frivolities or blasphemies were frowned upon by the stricter bodies such as the "Auld Lichts" and "New Lichts", of the Secession Kirk. They condemned to everlasting hell-fire all aids to harmony. But they often had a hard time to praise God in metre, let alone tune, if the precentor was unable to get his tuning-fork going, as often happened. And in the upland kirks where dogs outnumbered the Christians, canine choristers did not harmonise with humans.

A bright spark of humour luckily shines now and again from the gloomy archives of the ecclesiastic past. The Reverend Thomas Martin, who was presented by George III to Langholm in 1791, was a man of wit. During a discussion on Psalmody at the General Assembly he enlivened the debate by his proposal to make up a Musical Presbytery of the following members, whose names so suited their parishes that Heaven must have fore-ordained their ministries.

Singers of Fa-la .... (Rev. Arch. Singers............ 1753-1830)
Sangster of Hum-bie............................ (Rev. Henry Sangster......... 1738-1820)
Pyper of Pencaitland .... (Rev. David Pyper............. 1760-1813)
Lo-rimer of Haddington .... (Rev. Robt. Lorimer.......... 1765-1848)
　　　(Had ane tune)

DRINK

The earliest knowledge we have on fermented drink in what is now Scotland is to be found in that famous poem "The Gododdin" written in the time of Arthur by Aneirin, the old British or Welsh bard. It reveals that the court of Dunedin drank wine in plenty, as well as mead. The wine had been introduced centuries before by the Romans, but the mead had been longer known. They probably also had verjuice, which was a mixture of apple-juice (probably crab-apples) and honey. Ale is not mentioned, but it was commonly brewed by the Germanic tribes, Angles etc. so the Britons would know of it. But there is no mention of distilled drink such as whisky, brandy or gin though the Picts or Gaelic Scots could have made it, for their metal technique was of a high order, and a copper "worm" was not beyond them.

The lament at the end of the 13th century, "When Alexander our King was dead", shows that the mediaeval Scots enjoyed wine and ale, much of it imported. But whisky did not come to be popular in the Lowlands until comparatively recent times. It was made universally throughout Ireland and the Highlands long before the Malt Tax was imposed, following the unpopular Act of Union in 1707. The Highlanders, who ignored these foreign restrictions, continued to make it without permission until well into the 19th century. In 1851 one hundred gallons of "illicit" whisky came daily into Glasgow from the islands of Loch Lomond alone. Robert Burns was employed partly to put down this trade, over half a century before, and to prevent smugglers from landing cargoes on the Clyde and Solway coasts. The only family with permission to distil was Forbes of Culloden, makers of the famed Ferintosh; this was later withdrawn, occasioning the lament, the rhyming of which seems that of a man rather well on in his cups:

"O Ferintosh, o sadly lost."

Whisky, "Scotch," is made all over the world and is perhaps a boon, but there is little doubt that the Highlanders found it essential to their way of life; and, when snuff or "sneeshin" came in, their happiness was complete.

Very few Highlanders used whisky as an anaesthetic, but as a medicine, or aid to good fellowship.

"Have you ever seen Donald the worse of drink?"

"Ach no, But I've often seen him the better of it."

"Have you ever drunk bad whisky, Iain?"

"There's good whisky and better whisky but not such a thing as bad whisky."

A centenarian clansman was asked his recipe for centuries.

"Moderation in a' things, especially drink. I made twa rules for my guidance. Never to drink whisky withoot water, and never to drink water withoot whisky."

Taken separately they were classed as deadly poisons—by the Lowlanders. The Highlanders had a superstition, if necessity compelled them to drink water alone, without whisky, that it would do them no harm if they urinated at the same time. Prince Charlie habitually did this in the '45. Later in life he wasn't so particular.

The song, "Campbeltown Loch" probably was inspired by an old story. A drover was seen by the laird, drinking, on his hands and knees, from Loch Lomond.

"Man, Donal', tak it aff," cried the chief, meaning, drink the whole lot.

"If it was whisky, I wad do my damndest." was the reply.

A Highlander is rarely parted from his dram, but it sometimes happens.

Dugald used to call twice a day at a little riverside inn above Ballater, but in a spate of the Dee he was drowned above the inn, and his corpse carried some miles, to be retrieved below the town. When the innkeeper heard the news he remarked, "It just shows the dreadful effect of water on a man, for it's the first time I ever heard tell of Dugald Farquharson gangin' by the road-end, withoot comin' in for a dram."

It takes a lot to keep a man from his drink. A confirmed drunkard in olden times was described by his wife as "ane that could weel tipple drams, e'en gin they were dreept through a bedirten cloot."

A Glasgow wifie was tired of nagging at her boozy man and cleaning up after him so she determined to cure him once and forever. She told him before he sallied forth on Saturday that some night he could bring up his bowels when he vomited into the jaw-box. To drive home her point she gutted two rabbits and left the entrails in the kitchen-sink.

Next morning she confronted the offender. He was very subdued. "I'll never touch a drop again. Aillie. Last nicht it happened as ye had tellt me. But by the help o' God and a big spune I got them a' back again." She dared not let the cat out of the bag, or the rabbit.

The best old malt whisky is like nothing else on earth. But a Lowland gamekeeper thought there was something else which was equally agreeable though he had never actually tried it. On turning down an empty glass he remarked, "That gaed ower the pap o' ma hass for a' the warld like a cleckin' o' new-born kitlins."

A thirsty patient was prescribed one ounce of whisky daily, and absolutely no more. Luckily, he got out of this by recalling from his schooldays that an ounce consisted of sixteen drams.

"Whisky has killed countless thousands," said the temperance lecturer, to which the reply was, "I've never heard tell o' ony hard drinkers yet that whisky killed, though I've kent dizzens that dee'd in the trainin'."

But there is no disputing the fact that whisky drinking has been a great evil, since it left its Highland home and settled in the great cities and towns of the Lowlands. The cause did not lie in the whisky, which was a blessing among the Highlanders: the cause was the unbearable misery of life in the filthy rookeries of "industrial" Scotland, which drove folk to seek an easy escape.

Sheriff Alison of Glasgow said in 1851 that ten thousand men in that city got drunk every Saturday, stayed drunk all Sunday and Monday, and returned to work on Tuesday.

How different this was in the late 18th century in the same city, before the Hungry Twenties, Thirties, and Forties of last century. In Burns' time a common "pey-day" song was;
"O, this is Siller Saturday,
The morn the restin' day,
Monday up and tae't again
And Tuesday push away."

Two Glasgow cronies, after a drinking session, were helping one another home. One of them stumbled and fell. His friend looked about for him, and at last spied him on the ground.

"Eh, Willie, I wad like to lift ye up, but I haena the pooer. But man, I lo'e ye like a brother, and because I lo'e ye sae weel, I'll tell ye what I'll dae. I'll lie doon aside ye."

On a pouring wet Ne'erday night in Glasgow a celebrant fell into the reaming gutter. A constable loomed up and tried to lift him.

"Offisher, never mind me. I can soom. Help the weemen and bairns and them that canna soom."

Burns as a young man knew Douglas Graham of Shanter, a farm south of Ayr. He was the original Tam o' Shanter. Whisky and brandy were smuggled freely and Burns witnessed the entire household of Shanter, men, women and children, mortal drunk for two and three days at a time.

In the Borders, in Berwickshire, the "Drinkers of Sisterpath Mill" were proverbial. Ignoring the old proverb "It's lang or ye cry 'Shoo!' to an egg," they

32

sat down, in a mood of determining sociality when a "cloakin' hen" was set upon a clutch of eggs. They did not rise from their drink until the chicks were running about the house. That was at least three weeks. Burns did not exaggerate when he said, "They had been fou for weeks thegither".

Excuses for these bouts were many and varied.

The "Coo-couper" or cattle salesman of Swinton near Duns, used to complain. "Ye a' speak o' my muckle drooth, but nane o' my muckle thirst."

He put his muckle thirst down to the howdie, or midwife, having given him too much salt water to drink when he came into the world, it being the custom to give the infant only a sip of brine, to encourage it to give a little cough.

Secret and solitary drinkers are likely to be irredeemable alcoholics. Social drinking was and is more acceptable.

The factor of Jura was collecting his rents. A local worthy, Fleecy MacPhail, arrived with his rent and awaited the receipt. The factor wrote it out and as he handed it over he poured out only one glass of whisky and drank it, remarking, "You'll not be needing a glass, Fleecy." At which Fleecy helped himself to a good dram, remarking, "What is good for the factor of Jura will do no harm to Fleecy MacPhail." A sentiment with which no reasonable man will disagree. Fleecy's saying became a proverb.

But sociality alone was not the attraction. The very atmosphere of communal drinking was enough.

An old Irishwoman in Glasgow solemnly vowed to the father in the confessional that she would never touch gin again, but alas, she bumped into him one evening visibly intoxicated.

"Ah, Bridget, I'm grieved to see you have fallen from grace."

"Oh, father," she cried, "Heaven alone knows how hard I resisted. But tonight, it being the way the weather is, so wet and chill, as I was passing the open door of the pub, the smell of it passed upon me weary soul like the waft of a blessed angel's wing."

Probably one of the biggest factors contributing to the drink problem in Edinburgh was the very bad water supply before the Tweed reservoirs became available. Controversy, bitter and partisan, raged for years before anything was done, a state still prevailing on other matters. There were those who favoured St. Mary's Loch water, not on religious grounds either: some wanted draughts from Heriot Water, not because of old school ties: some Pentland, some Moorfoot, some Tweedside. Coloured magnifications of water-bugs, shrimps, fleas and snails appeared overnight on the billboards, supposed to put people off certain supplies. No wonder they were driven to drink anything but water or indeed anything from the tap, even infused.

Delirium tremens, or its lesser form, plain delusion, caused funny situations.

Deacon Dickson, staggering along, thought a high dyke had been built across the High Street during his hours in the howff, so he took a circuitous road home and only the clear air of the morning convinced him of his error.

For generations drinkers were warned to beware of "Deacon Dickson's Dyke"—a feeble joke indeed, backing up the English jibe, "If you want to make a Scotsman happy for life tell him a joke when he's young."

A party of otherwise respectable society ladies imagined the shadow of the Tron Kirk, cast by the full moon, was a deep stream, so they pulled off shoes and stockings, kilted their skirts, and waded across.

A famous and gifted Polish nobleman (a dwarf, only thirty-nine inches high), gave breakfast to selected guests in Edinburgh and conducted highly intellectual conversations with them. Nevertheless, the vulgar of the city, learning his name was Count Borowlaski, conferred on him the title "Barrel o' Whisky." (It may be of interest to those who delight in denigrating George IV, to know that he was exceedingly kind to the exiled Borowlaski in his extreme old age in London and visited him personally to enquire after his health and to take him gifts.) Despite his nickname, Borowlaski was a sober gentleman.

The most despised of men were those who fumbled while others paid. When a company gathered, often coming in at different times, it was the custom to go equal shares on the arrival of the doch-an-dorris or stirrup-cup (Gaelic: deoch-an-doruis). The modern habit of paying drink about, or round by round, is to my mind a social evil and it seems to me a pity that the "No Treating" order of the '14—'18 War was ever revoked.

Women were never allowed to "go Dutch" in old Scotland: indeed, in Holland, this is not a custom as far as I have ever seen. In Scotland the proverb was "Fair maidens wear nae sporrans," i.e. they were not expected to pay, though amongst the Newhaven fishwives, a distinct race apart, the women probably provided the cash; the final insult to a Newhaven woman was, "Her, she couldnae keep a man." On returning from a morning's sale of caller herrin, and other fish, in Auld Reekie, they usually had a drink, banded arms and filled the entire width of Leith Walk, about thirty or more yards, singing whatever marching songs occurred to them.

A gravedigger was well known as a tippler, which was excusable considering the nature of his trade. One day he rather overdid the drinking and was incapable of working, which, as it chanced, was very inconvenient, as his services were urgently required. The minister deputed the village doctor to visit him and give him some good advice, mixed with a little lecture on his behaviour. The doctor remonstrated with him on his back-sliding for a good ten minutes. Finally, when the 'bederal' could get a word in, he rounded reproachfully on his persecutor.
"Doctor," said he, "You and me has been in this parish for near thirty years, and in that time I hae happit doon a guid wheen o' your fauts and said ne'er a word about them to onybody. I think the least ye can dae in return is to turn a blin' ee to ane o' mine."

The "three bottle men" of old had a young lad to loosen their cravat, lest they choked when they slid under the convivial board. At one such drinking party several of the guests still remained seated towards midnight. The host looked at them one by one and remarked to his neighbour, "They're a' weel on, and merry, but what gars Garscadden look sae gash?" (ghastly). His boon companion replied. "He's been wi his Maker thae twa oors, but I didnae like to mention it an brak up guid company."

James Hogg, the Ettrick Shepherd thought that whisky was the key to immortality. He wrote, "If a body could just find oot the proper proportion and quantity that ought to be drunk every day, and keep to that, I verily trow that he micht leeve for ever withoot dying at a', and that doctors and kirkyairds would go oot o' fashion."

William Cowper describes an innocent winter evening:
"And while the bubbling and loud-hissing urn
Throws up a steamy column and the cups
That cheer but not inebriate, wait on each."

That may have been so in Merrie England, but away up in the Grampians in the Forest of Birse, it was a different story, for in this stern and picturesque land they brewed a cup that cheered and did inebriate. The well-known Birse Tea was fortified by liberal pourings of whisky. To this day when folk in the North are feeling the day has been too much for them, they make a pot of Birse Tea. No funeral was complete without plentiful supplies of hot Birse Tea, which even the teetotalers could drink with no remorse.

Animals are usually teetotal, but, in Scotland, there was a cow in Forfar which caused a lot of trouble in the law courts by drinking a whole tub of beer that a woman had set down by the door to cool. She claimed compensation, but it was finally decided that as the cow did not sit down to drink but drank at the door, standing up, it did not require to pay. The doch-an-dorris was always on the house.

Teetotalers were looked on in the old days with some suspicion. They were inclined to win converts from the whisky-drinkers.

A hardened boozer was persuaded, not only to give up whisky, but to lend his support to a teetotalist meeting by giving his testimony. The minister, who had got him to sign the pledge, introduced him and encouraged him to speak. He began: "I was aince a reg'lar whisky man. I had often a hale bottle at a sitting. Noo that I've stopped, I've been in better health, and I've enjoyed my meat mair, and forbye I've saved a guid wheen siller." (Loud applause.)

"Go on, man, you're doing grand," whispered the minister.

"In fac, freends, I've saved eneuch in the last month to buy mysel' a guid oak coffin wi brass hannles," (Cheers and applause.)

Thus encouraged the convert went on—"And I'll tell ye this in confidence, freends; gin I keep frae the drink for another hale month, by Goad, I'll need it."

The poor woman's husband had been on the bottle again and he was raving in delirium tremens. She was at her wits' end as the doctor was not nearhand. She thought, maybe it was more a job for the minister, so she sent for him. He came speedily and tried to sooth the fevered man; all that he could say was of no avail; the poor man kept crying out about the rats of all colours and conditions that were swarming up the bedposts to the ceiling. The minister rose to go.

"I'm sorry, it's no use my staying, my dear woman. What you man really wants is not a sky-pilot but a Skye terrier."

Here is a tragic Hebridean tale to end the chapter.

Old Ben Becula lay ill. "Tell the doctor to Coll." The doctor prescribed Rhum and Eigg. "Muck!" cried Ben "I'm Uist to a Mull of whisky and Iona bottle." "You'll Lewis your life," said the doctor. Soay did. They took him in a Barra to Skye.

CLOSED—
owing to
urgent pressure
of other business

SPORT

It may sound funny to say that if sport interferes with business you should give up business, but in Scotland, even among a people with a reputation for seriousness, it was almost an axiom. Some sports were so dependent on the weather that, if the climatic conditions were right, all business came to a standstill as everyone made for the open air.

Probably the most important of these sports was curling. Until quite recently, in historical terms, curling took place under natural conditions: that is to say, after several days of keen frost when ponds and lochs were bearing. Last century nature was assisted by the preparation of curling-ponds which were laid down on a level and covered with tar macadam or cement. They were flooded to a depth of a few inches and froze overnight, allowing a safe rink without delay. Inland villages, of high altitude, enjoyed a lot of curling each winter; but it was a sadder story for coastal places when it was known for several winters to pass and not a single stone thrown. But when a winter such as 1894-5 came along with over three months of hard frost, little work was done.

Here is a picture, in verse, of the scene when a severe and lasting frost drew out all the clubs from the Lothians and Stirlingshire to a bonspiel or great gathering

36

of curlers at an upland pond. I was a member for several years of the Buchan Club, probably the oldest in existence, and can vouch for the truth of the picture.

Ilk chiel that e'er had thrawn a stane
Twixt Pentland and the Ochils
Was oot o bed at skraigh o dawn
And lacin up his bauchles.

When a' the warld neath starry blinks
Lies dozin like a peerie,
Frae ilka airt a hunner rinks
Are heidit for Blaweary.

The dominie has left the schule,
The meenister his pulpit,
The miller-lad has quat his mill,
The collier his coal-pit.

There's some had stanes o reid Carsphairn
And some had channel yuckers
And some had casts o Carron airn
And some had Aîlsa chuckers.

I wadna care to multiply
Thae tales o curlin pliskies;
I ken we a' got mortal dry
And fell to drinkin whiskies.

There's some got fechtin fou that day,
And mony an ee was bleary,
But ane and a' got fell guid play
Bonspielin at Blaweary.

This was the old Scottish game of curling, the "Roaring Game," so called not so much because the players were encouraged to shout orders, or give encouragement, or applaud a good stone, as because of the roaring sound of stones as they sped over the ringing ice.

The modern game is standardised, from the weight of stones to the details of rinks, but the ancient game allowed all weights, shapes and materials of stones. The surface of the natural ice was often 'baugh' or partially thawed, or 'reuch' with snow and hail. Sweeping or 'soopin' had to be in earnest with a stout besom of brushwood, or tough heather.

Drams were essential to keep out the cold, and a fire, often a bonfire, was set going on the shore to heat up refreshments and spectators.

"In the deep mid-winter, long ago," I took part in a game at Longformacus in the Lammermoors. The countryside was deep in snow, owls screeching in the dark woods, and a full moon high in a cloudless sky. We had lanterns to guide us to the 'pot-lid', or bull's eye, and the ice was rough enough to separate the men from the boys. A magical scene.

That is where I learned a good trick which has fooled many a serious curler and driven him into hysterics. When a stone is obviously going too fast and will go 'through the hoose' I start to brush furiously behind it. This unusual play always attracts comment, and I explain by saying it is only logical, that if sweeping before a stone hastens its progress, then sweeping behind it must slow it down. Try this argument some time, and watch the reaction.

37

In "Rip Van Winkle" the Dutchman play ninepins without a sign of enjoyment or any emotion; Sully, a Frenchman, said that Englishmen take their pleasures sadly, but I know from experience that you can curl for three hours in Scotland and never get either a grunt or a smile, and yet at the end of an exciting game everyone agrees it has been most enjoyable. It reminds one of Thomas Carlyle's evening smoking with a friend. Not a word spoken, but a "wonderfu' nicht."

In golf the same taciturn mood prevailed. Near the end of an exciting but silent round, level-pegging up to the seventeenth green, the player who is one up remarks to his opponent, "Dormie," to which the other replies, "Chatterbox."

"Gowff" is more a drug than a pastime. An addict can think of little else, just like others who are "hooked" on their own special solace.

A golfer was holidaying at a Fife town, which naturally, was attached to a golf course. He sat one morning on a bench overlooking the links and got into a monosyllabic conversation with an old Fifer who was smoking a peaceful pipe.

"A grand view o' the Forth, man," he began.

"Aye."

"Awfu' times we live in."

"Imphm."

"A weel laid-oot coorse."

"Aye."

"Whit's bogey?"

"Fourpence an ounce. Man, it's daylicht robbery."

(Bogey roll was a brand of tobacco.)

A keen Scots golfer was voyaging to the States when he accidentally fell overboard in the dark. The liner went on and left him to sink or swim. He swam until he was nearly exhausted. Luckily his feet touched land and this inspired him to struggle ashore, where he fell senseless on the beach.

He awoke to find the warm sun shining upon him and a lovely sunburnt maiden smiling down on him. She told him she was so delighted at his appearance. She had been marooned for three years during which time she had seen no human being.

"Hoo have you survived?" he asked.

"By trapping fish and seabirds, and sowing and cooking oats."

"Oats?"

"Yes, several sacks of them were thrown up as flotsam. I sowed some and cooked the others. Would you like a bowl of porridge?"

"Porridge. Could I no'?"

She brought the porridge in a cocoanut shell.

"How about whisky?" she queried.

He could scarcely believe his ears. It seems she was a science graduate and knew how to distil.

He had a cocoanut shell of whisky and so had the lady.

"Would you like to play around?" she asked.

"Good Lord," he exclaimed, "Dinna tell me you've made a gowf coorse as weel."

I said gowff was a kind of drug, but in some cases it becomes a dangerous obsession. Neither money nor natural human affections deter the obsessed golfer.

The Fife song of last century describes a mild attack.

> Gowfin' a' the day,
> Daein' nae wark ava',
> Runnin' aboot wi a big bag o' sticks
> Efter a wee gutty ba'.

A "new-come gowfer" with all the latest panoply of war, brand-new outfit of every description, was playing with a native. He put down a new ball and hit it into the sea; his second attempt went over a boundary wall into a thick plantation; his third, too, was unlucky and disappeared in a jungle of whins.

"Why don't you use an old ball at a difficult hole like this?" his acquaintance asked.

"An old ball? I never have the damned things long enough."

From the depths of "Hell" came a sustained stream of oaths, broken by spouts of sand, as the erring golfer attacked the entrenched ball without effect.

"John, I don't mind for myself," expostulated his rather pious partner, "but I think there are some lady players coming within earshot."

"A'richt. I'll try to control my natural exasperation, though it's gey hard. I wish I had the deil that laid oot this bunker. D'ye ken, I began gowff as a decent Christian man, and it's fast turnin' me into a blasphemin' sinner."

On the same famous course two canny Fife professionals were playing for a wager. One of them drove too close to the railway line and landed in the thick 'fog' of grass and knapweed. He hunted anxiously, helped by his friendly rival. To lose the ball would cost him a stroke, which he couldn't afford. In depair he slyly dropped a fresh ball and shouted, "Here it is. I've fund it."

"Ye're a damned liar, Tam," said his opponent. "Your ba's in my pooch a' the time."

A worried man entered the fortune-teller's tent and sat down sighing.

"What can I do for you," asked Madame Stella.

"Weel, can your crystal ba' see what's hidden frae my een?"

"Yes."

"My wife has run awa wi' my best friend, God kens where."

"And you want me to consult the ball and ask where they are, I suppose?"

"Nae sic thing. I want ye to tell me whaur she pit my golf-clubs afore she left."

Death cancels all debts on earth, but not on the links.

A hardened pair of veteran players went out for a round, but at the 13th one of them collapsed and died. An hour later the greenkeeper saw one of them stagger up to the clubhouse with his pal over his shoulder. He rushed to help.

"It's ower late. He's past mortal aid. He deed at the 13th green."

"Do you mean to say you carried him all the way in? You're not a youngster either, John."

"O, aye, I cairret him. He was a guid freen o' mine. But it wisna his weicht I objected to. It was pittin him doon an' liftin' him up efter ilka shot."

Notable feats of strength, if not skill, have been performed in golf, very often unobserved or unpublicised. I once witnessed such a stroke during a competition at Craigentinny half a century ago. Among the competitors was the biggest man in the B division of Edinburgh police; a colossus of over twenty stone. Before a critical crowd he duffed his first drive, which rolled about a foot from the sand-tee. Blazing with Highland rage and mortification, he did not bother to re-tee, but smote the offending ball so hard and straight that he overdrove the green, over 300 yards, a feat never seen before or after. He would have been a terror with a broadsword.

Off the course some extraordinary shots were made both in the Old Town and the New Town. These are well authenticated.

James Grant's "Old and New Edinburgh" records a strange, almost incredible, feat as follows.

"In virtue of a bet in 1798, Mr Scales of Leith and Mr Smellie, a printer, were selected to perform the curious feat of driving a ball from the south-east corner of the Parliament Square over the weather-cock of St Giles's, 161 feet from the base of the church. They were allowed the use of six balls each. These all went considerably higher than the vane, and were found in Advocate's Close on the North Side of the High Street."

How this was done, one cannot imagine, for Dr Walker, a golfer of the time, describes golf-clubs as having "heads of brass, the face ... perfectly smooth having no inclination such as might have a tendency to raise the ball from the ground."

Early this century when there was very little street traffic, the stockbrokers and bankers in St Andrew's Square used to drive balls over the head of Lord Melville, whose statue stands 150 feet above street level. The number of windows they broke is not recorded.

Edward Topham, an English visitor to Scotland in 1775, seems to have gathered some weird impressions of the sporting prowess of the Edinburgh golfers, for he says that the summit of Arthur's Seat and other high hills around the capital were their favourite golfing places. Arthur's Seat, Edinburgh's tame volcano, is precipitous, and would defy the most agile of mountain goats, let alone golfers. As far as I know, golfers have not played on it. But in 1921, when I was a senior schoolboy, the maths master knowing I detested the subject, told me to take the morning off, and gave me a sixpence, to go by suburban railway to Duddingston to fetch his clubs. I bought a single ticket, and played my way back, illegally, across Arthur's Seat by St Anthony's Well; it *was* a rocky course, Mr Topham.

Golf is the ideal game for a metaphysical people like the Scots, who attack each problem as it arises, weigh up the pros and cons, and then take the appropriate action. Every stroke is a new problem, and the top golfers are known by their adaptability.

A true tale famous in the annals of St Andrews tells of James Braid, I think, who, at the 18th in a key game, was lying well over a hundred yards from the green, with his opponent level on strokes within puttable distance. A stiff east wind with drizzle was against Braid. After a moment's consideration, to everyone's dismay, he chose a baffie, a long-headed wood. He struck the gutty-ball with full force. It rose high and straight, caught the wind and dropped practically down the flag. His opponent, shaken, lost both putt and game.

Golf was still played on Leith Links in my grandfather's day. He lived nearby, and knew the special etiquette. A row of iron street gas-lamps lay across two of the fairways. If a golfer was unlucky enough to be fascinated by a lamp and smash the glass he had to go to the Leith Police office, in nearby Constitution Street, at the end of the game, and pay half-a-crown.

A lawyer, notorious for 'roasting' police witnesses, went into the charge office and was seen by the Highland sergeant in charge, who had suffered from his sharp tongue more than once.

"Weel, sir, what can I do for you?"

The lawyer banged his half-crown on the counter without speaking.

"What iss this for?" said the sergeant.

"Damn fine you know what it's for," fumed the legal man.

"I haf to be certain before I gie ye a receipt."

"It's for breaking a lamp," confessed the lawyer, irritated.

"Noo, let us be quite clear on this important point," pursued the bobby, enjoying himself. "Wass it the lamp you broke, or wass it the glass?"

This fine irony nearly produced a few apoplexies, since a number of fellow-golfers were in the background enjoying the scene.

Golfers may play single, from choice or necessity. Better to play alone than with an incompatible partner.

A pious person was playing by himself, partly because he did not like the strong language used by some club members. He was teeing up at the Rookery Hole when he saw another single approaching. He waited and suggested they join forces. This arranged, he went to address the ball, but after a preliminary swing he turned and lifted his club towards the heavens.

"What a lovely spring morning, my friend, nature awakening, and the rooks cawing in the trees. A marvellous symphony."

The other who was hard of hearing, put his hand behind his ear and cried "Eh?"

The pious player repeated his effusion.

The dour one, perhaps not on his game, cried, "I canna hear a word ye're sayin' for thae bloody craws."

Two casual acquaintances were perhaps luckier in their partnership. They had a drink before beginning their round. Their drives were good, approaches and putts almost incredible. They exchanged cigarettes and stories to their mutual satisfaction. To crown their morning's happiness two ladies appeared.

"Look," exclaimed one of them, lightheartedly, "My wife and my girl-friend."

"My dear boy," said the other, "You've taken the very words out of my mouth."

Golfers never prophesy, if wise.

A man with all the panoply of the game asked the caddie the name and length of the hole.

"The Tickly Knowe, sir, three hunner and fifty yards."

"Hm, a drive and a putt."

However the ball was topped and rolled sulkily a yard from the tee.

The only sound to break the heavy silence was the mutter of the caddie, "Noo for a hell o' a putt."

On another course a notice was displayed to this effect.

"Visitors are asked not to pick up lost balls until they have stopped rolling."

An equally incredible tale relates to the man who, to the surprise of his partner, appeared on the course equipped with a walking-stick. However, he was so expert he drove a beautiful ball with it, got out of a deep bunker in one explosive shot and sank a long putt.

His friend said, "Why don't you use golf-clubs?"

"Oh, I like to do everything the hard way. I encourage my family to do the same."

"How many children have you?"

"Two boys and three girls."

"That was good going. May I be so bold as to ask —?"

"No bother at all, dear boy. Standing up in a hammock."

Gowff has been played for centuries, on grass in Scotland, on ice in Holland. Styles have changed, of course, for in the middle ages clubs were often improvised. The old Scots game was played fairly low on the ground: it is interesting nowadays to see famous golfers use a putter from some distance on the fairway in the old style.

A whole vocabulary has passed away with the old tradition. Clubs no longer have names, even the holes are gradually losing their individuality. The Golf Museum in St Andrews commemorates the old game, and other museums are being set up in the States.

Gowff-bas were made of soft leather stuffed hard with feathers. It took a lum-hat-full of feathers to pack a ball. A special iron, with a small head, not much larger than a half-crown, was used to get a ball "out of a scrape", i.e. a rabbit-scrape. We must now leave the links for another national game.

Fitba or Fute-ball was like a free fight in former times. "Why former?" some cynics may say. The Scots proverb says "A' is fair at the ba' o' Perth." In many Scots towns, one end of the town played the other. Anything was allowed, as there was no referee, rules, time-limit or fouling.

An anonymous poet of the reign of James V described it,

The Bewties of the Fute-ball

Brissit brawnes and broken banes,
Stryf, discorde and waiste wanes,
Cruikit in eild, syne halt withall,
Thir are the bewties of the fute-ball.

which we could freely modernise as

Bruised muscles and broken bones,
Strife, discord and ruined homes,
Bent in old age and lame and all,
These are the beauties of the football.

History records that a team of Armstrongs, on their way from upper Liddesdale to play a football match, accidentally met Sir John Carmichael, Warden of the English Border. Words were exchanged, blows soon followed, and Sir John was slain in the tumult that ensued. Football hooliganism is not a new phenomenon. No wonder James VI wanted it "utterlie cried doun." He had

42

an ulterior motive. He wished the Scots to train for war but this was unnecessary because the kingdoms became united.

Blood sports were always popular, sad to say; and many of them were suppressed by law. These were bear or badger baiting, and cock-fighting. Wild boar, roe, red and fallow deer, were pursued by hounds and, in some accounts of these drives, hundreds were slain. The instinct which says "It's a lovely day. Let's go out and kill something," is still strong. And when the law can be broken at the same time it adds to some folk's enjoyment.

A notorious Border poacher was out early one day on the Teviot banks, with his muzzle-loader. He heard the quacking of wild duck so he hastily loaded his gun, forgetting in his hurry, to remove the ramrod from the barrel. He fired at the pair of mallard and secured both with one barrel: the ramrod as it fell transfixed a twenty-pound salmon which leaped clean out upon a sand-bank: Watty Scott himself got such a recoil from the effects of the ramrod's discharge, that he was thrown upon his back and killed a large brown hare in its form. So in one discharge of three drams of powder, he got two fowls from the heaven above, a beast from the earth beneath, and a fish from the waters under the earth.

This may seem like drawing the long bow but I can cap it with true poaching tales of my own, or friends' experience. A Border friend of mine, with two companions, many years ago cleeked ninety-six good salmon in Upper Tweed one evening, and laid them out in a sheep-stell. They took one or two and left word at a nearby hamlet where to find the others. As he tells it, "The folk had a reg'lar fit-path beaten oot to the stell afore daylicht."

A fisherman, hag-ridden, and never in a great hurry to leave the hotel-bar and his angling friends, was asked by his irate wife why he was so late in getting home. His excuse was that the salmon they caught was so big that they could not bring it home until a corridor train came along.

The story is told of the editor of a Scottish national newspaper who liked nothing better than a day's fishing in the Borders. He was enjoying a cast or two on a good trouting stream when a neighbouring minister, who recognised the editor, came down and got into conversation. After the usual enquiries about the kind of sport he was having, which bored the fisherman exceedingly, the minister, who was rather a pompous man and not at all a good preacher, announced rather grandly, "I, too, am a fisher, but I am a fisher of men,"

The editor thought it was time to deflate him, and get rid of him, so he said drily, "Aye, I had a keek into your creel yesterday, but ye hadna catched mony."

An unusual way of catching trout was practised on the Dye Water above Longformacus. The river flows in a very stony bed, most of the stones being flat. The fisherman carried a shepherd's satchel and a stone-breaker's hammer. He chose a stone likely to conceal a trout and gave it a sharp blow with the khapping hammer. This stunned the trout momentarily, and before it had time to recover he had it in his satchel.

The Highlandmen of old had a weird trick to drive salmon into their bag-net. They placed horses' skulls along the ways of escape. These ghost-like objects scared the salmon and directed them to their fate.

One of the oldest sports, still popular, is archery.

The principle is the same, however much the bows and arrows may differ; the sudden straightening of the bow, and tightening of the string, send the arrow off at a great speed.

In Galloway on the Black Dee, there is a farm called Craigancaillie, where Robert Bruce witnessed a remarkable feat of archery. A young man, to prove his ability shot at some ravens on the crag and pierced two with the same arrow. Bruce enlisted him immediately in his guerilla force, as a very useful follower.

Archery was a sport encouraged by law. Until guns became efficient, which was quite a long time after the invention of gunpowder, contests were carried out for prizes in most burghs by the local archers.

James V, in his poem "Christ's Kirk on the Green" tells of a tumult at a merry-making where the revellers began to use their bows and arrows, luckily with no serious results. One irate bowman, intent to slay, had his shot diverted over a roof-top. The report came that he had by chance killed a priest a mile off, at which he threw away his weapons and fled.

Everyone agrees that sport is its own reward and that incentives corrupt it, but all through the ages the natural sporting instincts of man or woman have been prostituted. In mediaeval times in Scotland, every man had to be ready to take up arms, for the Scots were out-and-out democrats, as they made clear in the Declaration of Arbroath, and would not tolerate employing mercenary troops, as many countries did. It was therefore necessary that sport should be a preparation for war and that feats of athleticism, of prowess with weapons and of skill in combat should be performed at gatherings.

Highland Games and Lowland Games alike were patriotic meetings, where marches, music, dancing and merriment made an annual highlight and drew great crowds to worship the heroes who ran, jumped, putted, threw and tossed. Our ancestors were like ourselves in their admiration of muscle-men. I have no space here to describe the mighty deeds of past and present, but those interested in these picturesque gatherings should read David Webster's "Scottish Highland Games", which gives all sorts of tales of mighty sports. The actual attendance at a Gathering, in a glen surrounded by wild bens and forests, with cloud, sun and showers flying, and the skirl of the pipes through it all, is, of course, an incomparable experience which outshines all written accounts.

The big day of the year, in many Border towns, is the Common Riding, when a party of horsemen and horsewomen ride round the boundaries of the common land to ensure the burgh does not allow its right to the land to lapse. In many towns, too, the Highland Games are the great annual event, and nothing on heaven or earth is allowed to interfere with them.

The story goes that a visitor to the Sports in a small Border village was rather surprised at the small attendance, both of spectators and competitors, and asked one of the officials why this was so.

"Weel, ye see, this is just yin o thae unlucky coincidences, It happens this year that oor Games fa's at the same time as the Olympics."

In Dumfries the "Siller Gun" was awarded to the winner of a shooting competition, but the annual event was marked by drinking and roistering. At one of the "Siller Gun" shoots the finalists were so drunk that they had to have their friends aim the guns for them, while they fumbled with the triggers. One winner, who hit the bull with the aid of his friends, did not know of his success till he sobered up the next day.

In 'Old Mortality', Scott described the sport of musket-firing at the Popingay or parrot, a bundle of coloured feathers hanging from a pole, which the competitors had to strike.

Jousting, a relic of the knightly combats of earlier times, was held too at these burgh sports. This was not a matter of life and death, but a comic affair, where the unwary rider was often unhorsed by a sack of sand which swung round and caught him in the rear.

Sport took many peculiar forms, At Stirling, there is a hill which is still called the Hurly-Hawkie, though the game which gave it the name has long since been forgotten. The boys and girls used to get cows' skulls with the horns still attached and slide down the very steep slope on them, with many a spill and thrill. A "hawkie" is a cow, a hurl or hurly is a ride. It was an all-the-year sledging game.

Dancing allows everyone to express himself (or herself) according to the mood of the moment. At the country 'hops' the master of ceremonies stood on no ceremony. It was often a case of "Drops o' Brandy! Grab your wumman!" and the devil take the hindmost.

At one such dance there were two very plain girls who, too often, had to be wall-flowers. The M.C. did his best to get everybody on to the floor, but he had a difficult job persuading any young man to take up either of the Miss MacPhersons. A reason could plainly have been found, for each of these nymphs weighed just over sixteen stone.

One night, the M.C., quite exasperated, approached a number of young lads, and used the local phrase for inviting a lady to dance.

"Come on, noo, dinna sit there a' nicht. Are nane o' ye gaun to *lift* the Miss MacPhersons?"

The village "hops" were primitive functions no doubt but there is no disputing that everybody had a roaring good time and thought they deserved it. Here is a verse to show the uninhibited nature of a Berwickshire country dance.

And noo the runnin buffet has at lang last a' run oot;
They've drunk mair beer
And whisky here
Than fill the Kyles o' Bute;
The hauf o' them are fechtin fu'
The tither hauf are fain,
They dance the Reel o' Tulloch
Till the sweit rins doon like rain,
Fu' saut this nicht.

Every form of sport lends itself to tall tales, but poaching, being illegal, and secret, provides perhaps the tallest of all.

When fishers gathered in such places as the Traquair Arms on Yarrow, many yarns were spun requiring a pinch or perhaps a peck of salt to help swallow them.

A salmon-poacher, for example, told how, having carelessly left his cleek at home, he improvised one from a green willow wand and a large fish-hook. The salmon he struck was so powerful it carried away the wand and hook. The following season he was out "burning the water" when to his surprise he saw a bush moving upstream. He pulled it out and found that it was growing out of a big salmon. His wand had sprouted and grown into a small willow tree. Baron Munchausen had better look to his laurels.

In a deep pool near a crook in Gala Water there lurked a legendary trout; it is said that angling consists of "a rod, a line and a fool at each end" but this old trout had a higher I.Q. than the anglers, and would not rise to any lure. However, one evening, a local angler saw a bum-bee floating down towards the pool where the veteran trout lurked. A splash and the bee disappeared. The fish had developed a taste for bees, so the angler caught one, and putting it on his hook, made a cast. The trout took it immediately and was pulled in after a long struggle. It was over seven pounds in weight, nor was that all, for when it was gutted it yielded two pounds of comb honey.

BEASTS

As everyone is aware, some of the higher animals have a sense of humour which they express by actions and signs. Apes, porpoises, dogs and crows clearly indicate that they enjoy practical jokes, but there is no proof that parrots appreciate the humorous sayings they are taught, or that laughing jackasses or hyenas enjoy a jest. Many humans, too, are devoid of humour. But the Scots pretty generally, being a philosophic people, associated practically all the animal world, from the smallest insects to the largest animals, with humorous incidents, or sayings, and put words in their mouths, also; which renders this chapter rather fictitious in places. We shall work our way from the lowest beasts to the highest.

Few creatures could be more poker-faced than oysters, which used to be very plentiful in the Firth of Forth and must have been present at the wittiest gatherings in Europe in Auld Reekie's howffs, though not in a humour to join in the fun.

Oysters were so greatly appreciated that Robert Fergusson honoured them with a whole poem to "Caller Oysters", which tells, among other interesting and humorous things, that they were in season when there was an R in the month.

Auld Reekie's sons blyth faces wear,
September's merry month is near,
That brings in Neptune's caller cheer,
New oysters fresh;
The halesomest and nicest gear
Of fish or flesh.

The Firth of Forth abounded in all kinds of sea-food. Fergusson mentions all the fish found there and does not forget lobsters and partans, or edible crabs. These shell-fish were, with herring, the staple food of the district. They are mentioned in many proverbs, along with other fish.

"Ye look like a runner," said the Deil to the lobster, referring to the lobster's eight legs and two claws. The lobster is actually the swiftest beast in the sea but it is his powerful tail that gives him the acceleration. In Aberdeen when a wee "loonie" has fat cheeks he is often called "partan-faced" for his features resemble the shell of a crab. Referring to the humble dwellings of the poor, it has been remarked, jokingly, "The ceilin' in their hoose is sae laigh that they canna eat ony fish but flukes."

The fluke, or flounder, is said to have so annoyed St Columba that he cursed it with a perpetually twisted mouth, when he landed in Dalriada (Argyll). Has this something to do with the clan Campbell for their name in Gaelic means "twisted mouth"? "Fluke-mooed" is not a compliment in fishing communities.

The scientific classication of plants and animals was not made until quite late in history, but our ancestors saw resemblances between land and sea-beasts. In old French a *poux* was an edible crab; on the Berwickshire coast to this day partans, or crabs, are sometimes called *poos,* the female being a queen and the male a cock. In modern French a *poux* is a louse or flea and an edible crab is a *crabbe,* though of a rougher and larger kind than a partan. A satirical English poet spoke of "The crab-louse with his bag and baggage." The two species are clearly associated as this story shows.

A boastful visitor to Lochaber was belittling everything in the district, so the Highland hotel maid decided to teach him a lesson. She slipped a large live crab into his bed. Before long, howls of agony were heard from his room.

"What's the matter? Are ye taen badly, whatever?" He pointed to the clinging crustacean. "Ach, is that all to be making a fuss over? That's just an ordinary Benderloch flea."

When men are in drink, whether the better or worse for it, they make mistakes and cannot differentiate "fish, flesh or good red-herring." An inebriated soul, thinking to himself proverbially "Eat-weel's drink-weel's brither" mistook the fishmonger for the pastry-cook and bought a bag of crabs, still warm from the boiling. He returned in a short time. "What's wrang wi' them?" demanded the shopman.

"Naething muckle wrang wi them. They're gey tasty pies and I'd like a few mair. But, if anything, I think they're maybe a wee thing hard in the crust."

The "halesome" herring, salt, kippered or fresh, was once the staple food of the poor. It inspired the majestic song by Lady Nairne "Caller Herrin" based on the Auld Reekie Fishwives' street-cry.

Another ballad on a lower key, "Tatties and herrin' " is very popular now with the media minstrels. It refers to the common method of preparing this dish by laying salt herring on top of potatoes and boiling the brine out of them. Herring dominated many regions of Scots life and are recalled in such lines as

"But the herring loves the merry moonlight
For he comes of a gentle (i.e. noble) kind."
and the West Highlandman's prayer
"If only the peats would cut themselves,
And the herring jump onto the shore,
Then I myself in my bed would lie
For ever and ever more."
                              Amen.
Not so well-known is the sarcastic Newhaven saying which, owing to the present dearness of the commodity, has lost its point.
"If it's to be a waddin', let it be a waddin'. Bring oot anither herrin'." i.e. Damn the expense, which was four a penny.

Eels are slippery customers and no fisherman who has caught one ever wants to catch another, after he has unravelled the unique slimy knots it ties around his line. When we were boys the favourite way to catch them, in the Water of Leith at "Puddocky", was to tie a few worms in a small ball of unravelled wool, and lower it into the haunts of eels. Their rows of hooked teeth got caught in the wool, and we just pulled them out and shook them off.

Eels were not much eaten in Scotland, either jellied as in London, or smoked as in Amsterdam. The "blue spaghetti" of elvers disgusted Scots. But a favourite moonlight sport was catching eels by torch-light with a pair of blacksmith's long handed pincers. They were popped into a sack and poured down the "lum" of a cottage, no doubt to the consternation of the residents for they can survive on dry land for hours and it was no fun to jump out of bed on to a mass of wriggling eels.

They were rarely eaten, but were flyped i.e. skinned, by being turned inside out. The tough skin was dried and made into whips, for "peeries" (tops), bootlaces, or even make-shift "nicky-tams" (ploughmen's trouser-leg garters).

Now we may progress to dry land, but first come amphibians. The commonest of these are newts, frogs (puddies), and tadpoles (powats, a pow being a head), and the "odious toad" whose tongue is the quickest thing in nature.

A Scottish soldier, with a bucket, was seen in a marsh in Flanders during the '14-'18 War. He was asked by a pal what he was doing with the bucket.

"Wan o' thae Froggy fermers wants me to fill it wi' puddies, and he'll gie me a soo, but the buggars keep lowpin' oot." On being told what a "sou" meant in Flanders he disgustedly "cowpet oot the puddies" and tossed the pail away.

Adders, like rattle-snakes, give warning of their intentions. Contrary to common opinion about them, they are not aggressive and will be quite pleased to wriggle away if unmolested. Yet they inspire a horror in many people. A postman friend of mine in the Lammermoor Hills, where notice-boards used to say "Beware of Adders", was once taking a short cut above a deep pool of Dye Water when he accidentally laid his hand on a coiled-up adder. Without hesitation he dived, letters and all, into the pool; he thought himself "between the devil and the deep-blue sea."

The Adder's Aith or Oath is a rhyme which was once believed in:
"I've made this Aith and I'll keep it true
I'll ne'er stang man through guid sheep's oo."

D   49

This may have been only a superstition. On the other hand, as woollen cloth was home-spun and fairly thick, it probably meant that the poison-fangs of the adder were not long enough to penetrate it.

Bees are in two distinct classes; those that work for us, and those that are self-employed. The self-employed are the humble- or bum-bees of which in Scotland there are five kinds, all prosperously fat with coloured hairy waistcoats. Cheeky Edinburgh bairns used to ask shopkeepers for "A bawbee's worth o' bum-bees' weskits." In the country the wild bees were called "foggy-toddlers" because they toddled on all-sixes through the foggage or moss into their small "binks", or bunks. The old drinking song "Toddlin' hame by the licht o' the mune" means that the inebriated ones went home on all fours, like a honey-drunk bum-bee going into its nest.

Hive bees on the other hand are managed for our profit, and it takes over two thousand of them, a whole summer day, to bring in a pound of honey.

A simple city lass had overheard people say "I see ye keep a coo" when butter or cream was on the farm table, so she showed her knowledge of rural life, when a comb of honey appeared, by saying "I see ye keep a bee."

A townsman was given the task of branding all the beasts belonging to a certain farm. In the evening the farmer asked him how he had got on. "Oh, no that bad, but I had an awfu' job wi the bees."

Before going on to the birds, I should mention the phrase "The birds and the bees". Their methods of reproduction if adopted by humans would lead quickly to the "Marriage Guidance Council" or the Divorce Courts, so perhaps the following tale from "Upland Aiberdeen" will point a moral.

The farmer attended a meeting in the village hall on "Sex Education" and had it all explained by the college lecturer. When he came home his teenage son was curious. His father satisfied him.

"Weel, Jock, d'ye mind last back-end when the twa dairy-deemies (dairy maids) cam up to the Mains to len' a haun at the hairst-time? D'ye mind what you and me did wi' them in the barn? Weel, the birds and the bees a' dae the vera same thing."

Geese, like ducks, are comical; geese in addition are as good as watch-dogs. They also used to be trained in Scotland for fishing, a baited line being tied to a leg and the gander put onto a loch. When a pike took the bait it was great amusement, for the spectators anyway, to watch the duel as the gander made for the shore.

James V visited the MacFarlane chief, and was entertained on an island on Loch Lomond. The tame geese were chasing one another all over the surrounding loch, amusing the king very much by their antics. A roast goose was served up at dinner, with other dainties, but the king found it very tough and passed this remark: "I see your geese like their play better than their meat." They got too much exercise to be tender.

As a small boy in the Vale of Leven I encountered my first bubbly-jock which liked not only its own meat, but mine. My mother had given me a hot boiled potato to eat, but the bubbly-jock eyed it and chased me on to a seat. Although I held it as high as I could, he pecked it out of my hand, so I have always had some sympathy with the mentally-handicapped lad who had been boarded on a farm as an "orraman." A welfare officer asked him if he were happy. He said he liked his food and lodgings and his Saturday sweeties. But in the end his secret terror came out. "Oh, mister, ma hale life here's made a misery. I'm sair hauden doon by the bubbly-jock."

Glasgow recently introduced farm animals into one of the city parks so that the citizens may be more familiar with the beasts. Last century there were many who had no opportunity to go into the surrounding countryside and see the wild beasts in their haunts.

A bailie, who knew nothing of Scottish fauna, wild or tamed, was trying a case where a man was sueing another for loss of some ferrets, due to neglect in closing the door of their cage.

The bailie summed up as follows, "I find ye baith responsible. The defendant shouldna hae left the cage open and the plaintiff should hae seen to it that their wings were clippet."

Some time ago I was showing the sights of Edinburgh to two Australian ladies. I mentioned in passing that the Edinburgh people had been very excited and delighted when the ·first Aussies arrived in 1915, wearing kangaroo's feathers in their hats (This was a First World War joke in Auld Reekie.) Neither of the ladies smiled. Then one remarked rather informatively. "But kangaroos don't have feathers". At which I looked as naive as possible.

The first time the old Scots lady saw a moose, she put on her specs to read the label on the enclosure. "Michty me." she cried, "A Canadian Moose. It's a guid thing there's a high fence roond it. Losh preserve me frae comin' face to face wi' a Canadian rat."

Much was expected of dogs in the way of intelligence.

A farmer was trying to drive a calf to market, and his dog was excitedly barking, as the calf wandered off the road.

"What are ye bowf-bowfin aboot, ye daft cratur?" shouted the man. "It wad be mair like the thing if ye was to gang and fetch a barra."

A shepherd in the Covenanting country was shouting to his dog when the minister chanced to pass. "Moreover, come about there. Moreover, come here, lad."

"That's a funny name for a dog," said the minister. "Do you not mean Rover? I never heard of a dog called Moreover."

"I'm surprised at you, sir," said the herd, "He's named after a dog in the Bible."

"I cannot recall it."

"O, yes. It's in the story of Lazarus. Moreover, the dog came and licked his sores."

The shepherd's collie is more than a match for most sheep, though the old black-faced ewes and tups often stamp at them defiantly.

At sheepdog trials astonishing feats are performed, but this shaggy dog story takes a bit of swallowing.

A stranger, wandered on the hills, sought shelter in a lonely cottage, and found the shepherd by the fireside, enjoying a game of draughts against his dog. The visitor watched with amazement as the collie made each move, even using two paws to crown his men.

"Man, that's a very clever dog you have."

"*Him* clever. The bugger's no' won a single game the nicht."

Foxes, or tods, are even more cunning than dogs. They never kill on their own hillside, but will travel miles to raid hen-roosts and duck-houses.

After a snowy night I spotted one, thirty feet up, in the comfort and safety of two pine trees blown over against one another. Hounds and hunters would have passed by, for there were neither scent nor tracks, and few men look for a fox in squirrel's territory.

Sheep are very important animals in Scottish economy, and it is well-known that when the feuding and risings were over in the Highlands, the former chiefs drove off their tenants in the notorious "Clearances," and replaced them with sheep, which were more profitable. Sheep, however profitable they may be, are not to be preferred to men, though in a well-known anecdote, a shepherd thought men were inferior.

A party of eminent Edinburgh lawyers were on an excursion across the Pentland Hills, when the easterly wind was driving the haar or sea-mist over the hill-tops. The black-faced sheep, not yet sheared, were lying on the seaward side of the hill, exposed to the wetting wind. A legal luminary remarked to the shepherd who accompanied them, "Look at these silly sheep. They're lying there exposed to this damned soaking mist. Now, if I were a sheep I'd lie on the other side of the hill."

The "herd" retorted grimly, "Gin ye were a sheep ye wad hae mair sense."

The sheep had not yet been sheared, and they were pleased to have a cool rain to soak into their overheated fleeces.

There are many good stories about pigs. There seems to have been a sort of love-hate relationship between the Scots and the "unclean" swine. The scriptures condemned the eating of their flesh but as one countryman put it, "There's nae mair hertenin' soond and smell than the sizzlin' o' hame-cured ham on a frosty mornin'."

One of my eminent clansmen was Queen Victoria's Chaplain, the Very Reverend James Urquhart Macgregor of St Cuthberts. He was handicapped by being bandy-legged, or crom-shankit, which necessitated his standing on a stool in the pulpit. But he more than made up for this weakness by his fiery eloquence. Frequently in his sermons the fury of his forensic power caused him to foam at the mouth, and bespatter his black beard and moustache. He often told these stories against himself.

Visiting a farm on the outskirts of his extensive parish of St Cuthbert's he had some queer experiences. Once, after announcing himself, the farm-wife commented "Come awa in. I didna ken the Store (St Cuthbert's Co-op Association) had a meenister o' their ain."

On another occasion the only occupant of a farm he visited was a wee lassie who was also unaware of his identity. She took him to see the farm animals. They came to the pig-sty where she placed two chairs, to enable them to see over the low wall. She told him the pigs were honoured by being named after the local ministers. "There's Souter o' Dalkeith, a fine sonsy beast. The wee hungry yin is the Free Kirk minister. But yon's my favourite, the wee yin wi the bandy legs, a' covered wi' black birse and slavers. Yon's Wee Macgregor o' St Cuthberts."

A good story comes from Ecclefechan; shortly after the death of Thomas Carlyle, a native of that village, an admirer of the "Sage of Chelsea," had travelled all the way down from London to worship at the birthplace of Carlyle. A rustic was driving a large sow along the street. The Londoner asked him to point out Carlyle's birthplace. The man indicated the house and asked "Which yin o' the Kerls was ye interested in?" Taken aback, the gentleman replied, "Why, Thomas, of course," "Tammas," said the pig-tender," I ne'er heard tell o' Tammas daein' onything byordinar. John was a doctor, but to my mind the pick o' the hale bunch was Sandy. He was the best breeder o' white pigs on this side o' Lockerbie and that's a guid sax mile." The sow turned up its nose proudly at that moment, no doubt.

Horses are teetotalers which in the pre-motor days saved many a man's life when driving home, but on one occasion they landed a driver in serious trouble.
The Lady of the Big Hoose, a strong temperance worker, habitually took an evening drive, and leaving the carriage, walked through the woods to rejoin the coachman after he had driven via the village, where there was the usual licensed hotel. One evening she said she felt tired and out of sorts, so it was a case of "Home, James, and don't spare the horses." But when the horses came to the hotel, they stopped as usual at the bar doors. The lady looked reproachfully at James who, glad to clutch at any straw, seized the whip and laid it on crying, "Drive on, ye leein brutes."

Caesar brought one elephant to Britain, in 54 B.C. on his second visit, so that the sight and smell of it would terrify the British cavalry, which it did. Elephants were still wonders in Britain for nearly two thousand years thereafter.
Just before the 1914-18 War, close to my second-cousin's farm of Sarkbridge, Gretna, there was a piece of wasteland on the Solway merse where travelling folk camped. A menagerie arrived late one evening. During the night the elephant pulled up his stake and ambled off looking for fodder. The next morning was rather misty when the farmer's wife went out to feed the hens. She came running in, excitedly crying, "Willie, Willie, come oot, come oot! There's a great muckle beast as big as the barn, in amang the neeps, pooin' them up wi its tail, and stuffin' them up its erse."

The most formidable beast is man, much more so than lions, tigers, or gorillas, which now have to be protected. This is not a new situation. In the ancient world there was a Caledonian tribe known as the Attacotti who inhabited the region of the present Strathclyde. They were so ferocious, and even cannibalistic that the Roman legions decided that as they couldn't beat them they had better join them; so they enlisted them to form a front line legion whom they sent into trouble spots when weaker units couldn't face it. A barely credible tale illustrates their ability to take on lions barehanded.
When the Romans were running short of Christians to feed to the lions they picked on a few Attacotti converts for the Coliseum. A couple of tough guys from the "Toon Heid" were selected first and sent into the arena where this conversation took place.
"Did I ever get tellin' ye aboot the wee Taliani tairt I was chattin' up last Setterday?"
"Naw, ye never spilt it tae me."
"Weel, I was makin' the ice-cream, when a rap comes tae the windae but—aw, hell! Here's the lions, I'll tell ye efter."

THE KIRK

There is a rhetorical question, "Which is the most important leg of a three legged stool?" This could have been asked about every parish in Scotland, where the whole community depended upon the minister, the doctor and the dominie in that order: at least that was the order of their salary or income. In theory, the minister did not occupy an exalted position; he received a "call" from the congregation and was voted for: but in practice he was a very prominent and powerful person, and very little that he did remained uncriticised. So there were innumerable amusing stories about kirks and ministers; though many have little or no foundation. But in the "pawky" atmosphere of rural Scotland, where the minister did not always bother about decorum, many are well-founded. Some of the parishioners were pretty ignorant about theology, too.

On Sunday when the kirk was "skailing" old Davie, who had not attended that day, asked his crony as he approached,

"Weel, what was the meenister on, the-day?"

"Man, his text was frae the Proverbs aboot the wiles o' the deceitfu' woman, and frae that he wannert on to fornication and whoremongers."

"O, Sandy, I missed mysel. I should hae been there. Hoo did he treat the subject?"

"Man, he fair shook me. D'ye ken, Davie, he was deid agin it."

But in an upland parish a minister very unjustly got a reputation for fornication. To keep the congregation well up in doctrine he regularly went round the outlying farms, where all the locals gathered in the kitchen to be questioned on the "Carriches" or Shorter Catechism.

When he was crossing the muir at a lonely place, he was surprised to be met by a young farmer's wife carrying a basket.

"You are a long way from home, Mrs Bruce."

"O, aye, meenister. I cam ower to gie ye this bit o' butter and a few eggs."

"That's very kind, very kind indeed."

54

"Weel, sir, in return, seeing I've a very poor memory, will ye gie me a simple question this efternoon? I dinna like to be affrontit afore folk."

She was assured on this point.

In the afternoon it came to her turn and he asked her simply to name the seventh commandment, condemning adultery.

She stammered, her face reddened; she just couldn't remember. Finally, in her embarrassment she exclaimed,

"O, meenister, after what passed between you and me on the back-muir the-day, I little thocht ye wad hae askit me that."

A more guilty party was the minister who was right royally entertained at the manse of a colleague. After a grand supper, with plenty of the "Auld Kirk" to wash it down, he staggered upstairs to bed. In the absence of warming-pans, it was the custom to get a serving-lass to lie in the bed for an hour or so, before the guests went up. But this evening the big country lass, dead-tired, had fallen fast asleep. When the guest opened the door and his eye fell upon her, he stood and apostrophised the manse.

"Manse o' High Newton, ye've dined me weel, and ye've wined me weel, but this! This is indeed the heicht o' hospitality."

Some ministers had enough of the Old Adam in their make-up to get a kick out of shocking the prudish folk. One of these was Queen Victoria's Chaplain, the famous Dr Norman MacLeod.

On the long journey up to London, first-class of course, a young lady of fashion, aristocratic, was the only other occupant of the compartment. She disdained his efforts at polite conversation. In due course she fell asleep and soon after, Dr MacLeod dropped off too, and the book on which was written his name, fell to the floor. This woke her up. She picked it up and was gratified to find who her travelling companion was. When he awoke she exclaimed enthusiastically that she would be able to tell the fashionables, in her church in London, that she had travelled with the great Dr Norman." He smiled and said with a gracious nod, "Tell them also, dear lady, that you slept with the Great Dr Norman."

The seventh commandment seemed to have a great attraction for both ministers and parishioners, as it still has. In a parish, where there were a few well-known breakers of it, the minister had a habit of glaring at the more notorious as he preached on it. As the congregation went out, he followed this up by accosting these sinners at the doorway, and passing broad hints to them in a loud voice. To one hardened sinner, a hearty farmer, he said, "Weel, Maister Black, I hope ye got some benefit from my discourse."

"O, to be shair. Baith spiritual and material, meenister."

"The spiritual I understand, but I cannot understand how you got material gain."

"O, aye. In the middle o' the sermon it cam to me suddenly where I had left my best umbrella."

The minister and his wife were never suspected of being uxurious, as that would have been an unforgiveable piece of levity, however young and desirable the lady of the manse was. One minister in the severe days of religious bigotry shocked his colleagues by confessing, in his old age, that in his prime, he had helped his wife to conceive between the forenoon and afternoon sermons.

A young divine and his bride were asked to spend their honeymoon at the laird's "Big Hoose", where everything was on a princely scale, including the bed they had to occupy, which was about as big as the "Great Bed of Ware."

In the morning their host asked how they had slept.

The bride blushed. "O vera weel, laird, but in the middle o' the nicht I lost the meenister."

A bachelor minister was always at risk, for many a woman's ambition was to be mistress of the manse. There is usually a very good reason for the minister remaining a bachelor well beyond his youth. He may be an enthusiast for some hobby, and have no time to bother; though how a minister could adequately fulfil his duties without a wife, was beyond many folk's understanding. It was almost the rule for ministers to marry within their profession, so essential was it that the lady should know how to run the manse.

A middle-aged minister had a devoted housekeeper, still nubile, but he did not seem to notice her attractions, for his hobby was keeping poultry. She helped to look after them.

One spring day she returned from gathering the eggs.

"Hoo mony eggs the day, Janet?"

"Sixteen."

"H'm, sixteen." He did not seem very happy.

The following day he asked the same question and got the same answer.

"Ah," says he, "But I hae ye this time. I've turned them a' up and lookit at them. There's a full score o' them on the lay."

She drew herself up angrily.

"Then ye can just take my notice."

"O, Janet, ye canna leave me like that efter a' thae years. What is your real reason?"

"Weel, to be truthful, it seems to me it's the hens in this hoose that get a' your attention."

They were married not long after.

Hens take a good deal of studying. They have their own peculiar habits, which everyone in the country is supposed to know.

The minister was staying at a local hotel, and on retiring for the night, he found that he had not been supplied with a chamber-pot.

He went to the head of the stair.

"Mistress."

"Aye, sir, what is't ye seek?"

"Woman, d'ye think I'm a hen?"

In the pulpit things were on a different footing. The minister was sometimes momentarily carried away, and put himself on a par with deity.

Predestination was a minor belief of the Calvinists. It had been preached first by Augustine, but it worried many people to think their future was already blue-printed, no matter what they did.

"The maist o' ye in this kirk this morning are heidit straicht for hellfire," shouted the preacher. The congregation took this news calmly, as they had got accustomed to it.

As he spoke, a fat bluebottle buzzed up and sat upon the open page of the pulpit bible. The minister thought he would bring a touch of realism to the occasion.

56

"Aye, hellfire. Ye shall suffer the torments o' the damned, as surely as I shall ding the guts oot o' this muckle blue flee."

He raised his hand to smite Beelzebub, the father of flies, but the fly had seen the shadow of destiny, and as the heavy hand crashed down it took off and was airborne.

The frustrated predestinarian glowered at the poker-faced pews.

"Eh," he said, "There's a chance for ye yet."

On a visit to a local gardener the minister remarked on the fine crop of apples.

"Why, Thomas, this is like the Garden of Eden. Look at that lovely tree of the knowledge of good and evil."

"Aye, it bears gey weel, considering the cauld spring."

"Have you every thought of our first parents Adam and Eve?"

"Aye mony's the time. I aye think that gin I had been Adam the history o' mankind wad hae been muckle happier."

"You surprise me, Thomas. How could that have been?"

"Weel, sir, to tell ye the honest truth, I was never muckle taen up wi aipples."

In a long spell of bad weather the minister offered up prayers every Sabbath for a break in the storms, but week after week the wind and rain continued. On the fifth Sabbath his prayers were long and desperate. There came a sudden lull in the storm, and he thought this would be a good place to say Amen. But no sooner had he said it than a terrific blast blew in the west window.

"O Lord," he cried, "This is perfectly rideeculous."

But gratitude for good weather was not wanting, and the minister in a Northeastern parish was thanking God for a bountiful harvest of wheat, oats, barley and bere.

"We thank Thee, Lord, for this great gift. The grain is full in the ear, and a guid threty bushel to the acre. And a' are ripe unto harvest, except twa-three fields at the back o' Stanehive, scarcely worth the mention."

Sometimes the learned divine let a difficult expression slip out, which was above the heads of his hearers. He forgot whom he was addressing on one occasion.

"We thank thee, too, O Lord, for our economical superfluities, by which I mean, O Lord, these creature comforts we hae mair o' than we require."

Sometimes the minister would address the mighty dead in an aside, a stage whisper.

The subject was King David, a favourite Biblical hero, despite his human failings. His killing of Goliath never failed to get enthusiastic support, and many people were ready to believe that the famous last words of the Anakite were, "Sic a thing as a chuckie-stane never entered ma heid afore."

But this Sabbath the text was "And I said in haste 'All men are liars.' " "In your haste, Dauvit," said the minister, "In your haste. Gin ye had lived in this parish, ye micht weel hae said it at your leesure."

Reflections upon all sorts of "sacred cows" came from the privileged pulpit prayers. Even the General Assembly was not spared on one occasion when a cautious old minister in Edinburgh annually put up this special plea for them, "O, Lord, in thy wisdom, guide the footsteps o' oor General Assembly, and see to it that this august and reverend gathering, under your gracious hand, will dae nae harm."

Princes and potentates were not spared either. When Cromwell attended divine service in the High Church in Glasgow in 1650 the minister opened the vials of wrath upon him and denounced his character, his looks, his actions, his cause, sparing no curses upon the "Protector". One of his officers asked permission to go up to the pulpit and pull the minister down by the ears, but Cromwell told him he was one fool and the Presbyterian preacher another. Cromwell later held a peaceful conversation with the minister and they parted friends.

When the minister went visiting he often met an amusing adventure. He was usually offered a refreshment, either whisky or tea.

A very outspoken old lady was entertaining her preacher, a portly little man, not an eloquent preacher. He offered to pour out the tea, but unhappily he spilt some over the tablecloth. He apologised profusely, but the lady assured him there was no need. "It's no' your faut, meenister, it's the faut o' that auld tea-pot o' mine. It's gey like yoursel. It's a gousty wee thing, but it has an unco puir delivery."

An assistant minister in Central Glasgow last century was called upon to visit one of the congregation in a poor tenement in the Trongate. He was conducted to the ill man's bed-chamber and asked his guide why, as the man was extremely ill, they had not sent for the minister himself. "What, send for the famous Dr. — —. Certainly not. This is a very infectious case of typhus."

Certain ministers were considered expendible. A young clergyman had received a call from a parish, and had been enthusiastically voted in on the strength of his trial sermon. But, alas, he did not live up to his promise in any direction, so after due delay, he was discreetly told that he was no longer acceptable. As he left the manse, the 'minister's man' remarked to him, rather unkindly, "Aye, ye cam unanimous—and ye're gaun unanimous."

These first testing sermons were tests also of the minister's nerves. A young candidate for an important church was met and led into the vestry by the beadle, who poured him out a good dram. The young man expressed surprise. "Tak it afí. It'll steady your nerves, sir." Then, when about to mount the pulpit, he was offered another with the remark, "The last man aye took one. It gied him courage to face the folk."

The service went on like a house on fire. The candidate had never preached better. The congregation caught his enthusiasm. Now it came to the dismissal hymn, which the preacher announed in these terms. "We shall conclude by singing Hymn No. 663, and you can sing it to any bloody tune you like."

A professor of divinity with a pretty barbed tongue was giving a final advice to his students on how to become popular preachers. He described the most "eloquent" preacher in Edinburgh, whose kirk was packed to the door twice a Sabbath to enjoy an emotional sermon.

"He jumpit and joukit, yerkit and squealed for a' the warld like a roupy cock. Then he dozened doon and began to gie a bit greet. Aye, lads, that's the secret Get up a bit greet . . . and your fortune's made."

There was always a kind of rivalry between the "Wee Frees" and the Kirk of Scotland. A crofter member of the parish kirk was worried about his young turnips which were wilting for lack of a shower. His own minister's prayers for rain had not been answered. A neighbour gave him this advice.

"You should sink your pride, Sandy. Gang ower to the Free Kirk meenister and ask him to put up a prayer. Ye ken he has a great spate o' supplication."

"Maybe he has, whatever," was the reply. "But it's no vera likely he would be asking for rain for my neeps, when his ain hay is no in yet."

In many a pastoral parish there was a fence inside the Kirk to separate the devout from the dogs, for most of the congregation, in parishes like Heriot in the Moorfoots, or Cranshaws in the Lammermuirs, were shepherds. The "dog-end" had often more occupants than the pews, and occasionally when a fight arose, the preacher had to interrupt his sermon. Often, too, if the precenter hit the right key, which he sometimes did, the dogs would sit up and join in. In a Highland kirk, towards the end of an interminable prayer, a large stranger dog walked in looking for a fight. The minister had no time to say Amen, so this order to his beadle was included in the prayer.

"Lachlan mor, cuiridh a mach an cu, Amen."

(Big Lachie, run that dog out of the door, Amen)

Ministers were good at repartee and sharp reproofs. When the "Toon Cooncil" was being "Kirked" the minister saw that many of the magistrates were fast asleep, so he cried in a pulpit whisper. "Bailie MacNab, dinna snore sae lood. Ye'll waaken the Provost."

The "Minister's man" was often a bit of an ogre, and even the minister himself was afraid of him. One beadle became so impertinent and aggressive that the minister's wife got her husband to go and give him a good telling-off. When he returned she asked if he had been firm.

"Yes, my dear, I showed him my displeasure in no uncertain way."

"What did you say?" she persisted.

"I said to him, 'John, John', and many other harsh things."

The old classic, well-known, tells of the days when deaf-aids took the form of large ear-trumpets. An elderly lady armed with one of these had got settled down in her pew when the stern beadle crept up to her and uttered a threat which rang through the kirk, "One toot, and ye're oot."

A Highland minister used to go from Mull to preach on the tidal island of Gometra, which was, of course, cut off at half-tide. He took a very long time over the final prayer, which was interrupted by a loud whisper from the beadle who had accompanied him from Mull.

"Facal ann, a Mhaighstir Iain, 's am Brugh a lionah."

(Get on with it Maister Iain, the channel is filling.)

The minister on his many visitations had to be prepared to meet many embarrassing moments, which must have tested his Christian charity to the utmost.

When Sabbatarianism was rife, a very rigid minister called on a lady unexpectedly on the Sabbath, to find the girdle over the fire, obviously ready for a baking of scones. He eyed it severely, but before he could pass any comment, she had whipped it off to the pantry, remarking,

"Ye've nae idea what a damp hoose this is. I was just airing the girdle."

The "Life of Wallace" used to be a very popular volume and many houses had a fine volume bound in morocco so that it resembled a Bible. One enthusiast in Renfrew ordered a copy and was asked if he would like it bound in morocco.

"Na,na," says he, "Dinna gang to a' that bother. I'll just hae it bund in Glesca, like a' the ithers."

The Sabbath was not made for man in the Presbyterian country. Strangely enough, at that time, there was a proverb "The Sabbath never comes abune the Pass o' Ballybrough," meaning no one kept the Sabbath in the Highlands. Now the position is reversed.

Unbelievably this true story befell an Englishman in Edinburgh at the beginning of last century. He found that there was no form of public entertainment allowable in the city on Sunday; however, he was told, that if he went up to his bedroom, a girl would be sent up. She arrived and began to strip. So did he, almost incredulous but cheerful. He began to whistle, and was surprised when the lady put on her dress and made for the door, informing him that she refused to go to bed with a man that whistled on the Sabbath.

The minister had to answer some awkward questions on Scripture, such as "There's a thing I could ne'er remember. It's aboot Sodom and Gomorrah. Did they ever get mairret?"

Or again, to the preacher who often referred to Anti-Christ,

"Ye've no spoken aboot Annie Christie for a while back. Is she aye weel?"

Patience, even Job's, can stand only so much.

A couple presented themselves at the manse to have the marriage banns called, but the girl stopped the interview, saying, "It's off. I've ta'en a scunner at him." On the second occasion it was the man's turn. He had taken a scunner at the girl. However the couple turned up a week later appearing reconciled, but the minister met them at the door. "Ye can turn and go back the way ye came, for I've ta'en a scunner at baith o' ye."

Gretna in the wicked past was the despair of the parish minister. A number of idle parishioners fired muskets at the house-martins' nests under the eaves of the church. The powder set the thatched roof on fire and the kirk was destroyed. The wretches fled and left no addresses. The minister addressed a verse to himself.

"Arise, O James,
And save from the flames
Thy people who are sinning:
Angels, declare
Me who they are,
It's time I were beginning."

But no angelic "nark" appeared in answer to his call.

Forfar was another wicked parish. One old minister, preaching on the subject of Satan's temptation of Christ on the mountain, remarked aside in a stage whisper,

"My friends, when Satan showed oor Lord the kingdoms o' the earth and the glories thereof, ye may be certain o' this. He keepit his thoomb on Forfar."

60

The driver of the Aberdeen to Fochabers coach was no doubt a hard-tried man. He had driven in all weathers, through summer heat and snow storms, when the north wind came tearing like a wild beast through the Glens o' Foudland. His language was what was to be expected, but luckily the horses whom he addressed, if they understood the blasphemies, were not able to repeat them. On one journey a minister, travelling on the box, could keep silence no longer after a spate of expletives from John.

"Man, man, ye shouldna sweir in sic a manner, nae maitter though ye hae trials and tribulations. Job had sair troubles, but he had patience through them a'."

"What bloody coach did Job drive?"

The biblical text "Many are called but few are chosen," has been twisted about in Scotland where cauld means the opposite of warm. The Highlander, his kilt blowing about in wintry blasts, was supposed to complain. "I'm cauld wi the kilt and near killt wi the cauld," to which his friend replied, to cheer him up, "Many are cauld but few are frozen."

A minister was having a play of words with a witty parishioner one frosty morning.

"Vera cauld, meenister," remarked Sandy.

"Aye, it is that, man, but ye ken the saying, "Many are cauld but few are chosen."

"Ay, I ken it fine, but a theologian like yoursel maun ken that, if ye're no chosen, ye'll no be lang cauld."

When the Scots could joke about hell-fire, its terrors had gone.

The early Kirk records (18th century) of Minnigaff, when religious intolerance by the Presbyterians was most severe, give some ludicrous instances of petty tyranny, not only for alleged fornication, but for Sabbath breaking. A shepherd and his wife were haled before the session for "tedding" hay on the Sabbath. They lived at the "Laggans" about seven miles from the nearest house. Their plea was that they thought it was a Saturday and had no means of finding out otherwise. Yet they were assured that the Almight knew. Fined, and told, "Weel, ye ken noo."

A belief was firmly held that when the new kirk of St Vigeans was built it was supported on iron bars over a bottomless lake, this trap having been set by a water-kelpie who had carried the stones for the building of the kirk. From 1699 until 1736 no minister could be induced to hold communion in it, and if he had, he would have had no communicants, for all believed that the holy sacrament would cause the iron bars to give way. However, in 1736, a bold clergyman prepared the communion table, while hundreds of the parishioners sat on a hillock, a hundred yards away, prepared to see the kirk plump into a yawning gulf. However all passed off without the trap-door opening, and normal service was resumed.

A band of Westland Whig sermon-tasters were wending their way home, discussing the afternoon's preaching.

"Eh," exclaimed one enthusiastic wifie, "When yon haly auld man spak aboot Gabriel, and the host o' angels clappin' their wings wi' joy tae the soond o' the gowden harps, it fair gaed to ma hert, and minded me o' oor geese at

Clashgulloch, pittin their nebs intil the sooth wind and rain, when the Stinchar comes doon in a muckle spate."

The minister of a rural parish wanted everybody to attend services. He asked the gamekeeper if he could not be persuaded to come to church.

"Nae offence, sir," said the gamekeeper, "I wad like fine to come for I wad enjoy the service, but I dinna want to empty your kirk."

"How would your presence empty the kirk?"

"Weel, to be perfectly truthfu', sir, gin it was kent that I was to be in kirk, the maist o' the male congregation wad be oot poachin'."

The parish minister, a most eloquent preacher, with a great spate of sermon and prayer, met a travelling piper on the road. Jocularly he inquired, "Well, Iain, how well does the wind pay these days?"

The piper slyly replied, "You have the advantage of me on that score, your reverence."

AULD NICK

In Scotland, strangely enough, people believed in a single devil who went under many names such as Clootie, Auld Hornie, Auld Nick, Bob Mahoun. He had the power of appearing under various shapes and in many places. He could summon meetings of witches and wizards and take part in their wicked rites. In short, he was a very gifted and energetic personage, rather like a Moderator of the Infernal Assembly.

Now this was all contrary to orthodox views on demonology, a subject which received much attention over the whole Christian era, not only in Europe, but in the Muslim world. I have not space to do justice to mediaeval demons; my purpose is to deal with curious and amusing Scottish tales of devilry.

For any reader who wishes to carry research deeper, I recommend the "Discoverie of Witchcraft" by Reginald Scot, who did not believe in the existence of witches, but exposed the nonsense of all such superstitions. James VI was so angry at Scot for spoiling one of his favourite blood-sports (witch-hunts) that he ordered all copies of Scot's book to be burned. However, some copies survived and may be read in their original form.

Scot deals in great detail with the whole subject. Some of his phrases are quite comical as when he says of a certain school of demonologists that they resemble "babes fraied with bugges," not what it seems to mean to us, but "children frightened of bogeys."

The Damnation Army was as well organised as the Salvation Army, or any other. Zimimar was the lordly monarch of the Northern Division: Gorson, of the South: Amaymon, of the East: Goap of the West. The Commander-in-Chief was Lucifer, with 24 hundred legions of devils. As a legion of devils consisted of 6,666, Lucifer alone had 15,998,400 devils at his back. These devils could assume the faces of leopards, bulls, dragons, bears, serpents, cats, unicorns, night-ravens, branded thieves, or griffins.

With this wealth of demonry to choose from, how did Scots come to settle for such a simple "bugge" as a "black man with cloven feet, a pair of hornes, a taile, clawes and eies as broad as a bason"?

The fairies, dwarfs, elves and brownies were of a different breed. They were supposed to be of Teutonic origin, and could be good or evil impartially, just as it occurred to them. They were "kittle-cattle,"

A poor Scots wifie, Alison Pearson, was burned for witch-craft in 1586, not for communicating with the Devil but with the fairies. She confessed to holding conversations with the Queen of Elfland and the "good neighbours."

She suffered from a partial paralysis, and occasionally the fairies would gather herbs and brew them into salves to help her. In return she had to swear not to tell about them, or they would murder her. In the eyes of the witch-hunters, the fairies were just as evil as Auld Nick.

In fact, although the Devil was one personage, the whole of Scotland was so crowded with elves, kelpies, and brownies, that not a wood, river, spring or mountain was free of them. Satan wisely kept to places in the Lowlands, like Berwick Law, or Spott, or Tantallon, where he had room to swing his forked tail.

As time went on, belief in devils and elves dissolved and they became figures of fun, though, after dark, country folk were probably loath to visit kirkyards, and ruins "nodding to the moon." It was acceptable for Burns to make a humorous epic out of Tam o'Shanter's imaginary visit to Alloway's auld haunted kirk, or to address the Deil as an old crony. Yet at the same period as Burns' Tam o' Shanter nearly every household had copies of Dr John Brown's Bible Dictionary, wherein he recommended that witches "ought to be put to death; but great caution is necessary in the detection of the guilty and in punishing them lest the innocent suffer," as many instances in New England and other places show. The last witch was burned in Scotland in 1722 just a generation before Burns was born.

The devil was half-believed in, but folks were more inclined to treat him as an old friend than an old enemy. A proverb runs:
"It's aye guid to be ceevil,
Quo' the auld wifie when she beckit to the deevil."

The tale is told of a good church member who was of such a sweet disposition that her niece said to her, "Auntie, I believe you are so kindly natured that you would let Auld Nick into your pew."

"What for no?" replied the old lady, "Gin he wad only sit still and behave himsel."

To this era of doubt in the devil's power to do evil, also belongs the saying, "Ye wad dae little for God an the deil was deid."

They even began to take the mickey out of him as in such sayings as, "Are ye no a bonnie pair?" as the deil said o' his hoofs. or "Hame's hamely," quo' the deil, when he found himsel in the Court o' Session.

It is of passing interest that the reason for the Deil's horns and hoofs is to be found in Jewish writings.

The "scape-goat" was ritually laden with all the sins of the people and driven off into the wilderness; the goat was most often the form assumed by Satan in his meetings with his followers, as may be seen in Spanish and other European paintings of witches' sabbaths. The "harmless necessary cat" too was associated with witches and devilry, and had to share the tortures of poor demented humans. Cocks, owls, bats, serpents and toads were also drawn into a quarrel, which was not in the least of their making.

64

Any man of ingenuity or any woman who, by dint of genius and perseverance, was able to achieve work far above the ordinary, was immediately suspected of being in league with satanic powers.

John Napier of Merchiston, inventor of logarithmic tables, had the name of being a magician in league with Auld Nick. His life-story requires a volume to do it justice, but a bare outline of the more remarkable facts is interesting. When he was born, in 1550, his father was only 16; which rather destroys the idea that geniuses are usually bred of mature parents. The Reformation, and the civil wars which raged around Merchiston Castle, along with the terrible plague of 1568 were largely avoided by Napier, who at that time was studying on the Continent after graduating at St. Andrews.

Two amusing tales of his association with the Evil One were long remembered. He had a jet-black cockerel which, because of its colour and its association with cock-crow, was regarded with awe. The crowing of a cock was the signal for ghosts to return to their lairs. In the "Wife of Usher's Well" this verse is spoken by the ghost of one of her sons:

"The cock doth craw, the day doth daw,
The channerin worm doth chide
Gin we be mist oot o oor place
A sair pain we maun bide."

A theft of valuables had been committed within Merchiston Castle, so Napier decided he would find the thief, and ensure against future trouble. He ordered his servants one by one into a dark room in the tower where the cock was perched. He told them beforehand that the cock had supernatural powers, and when stroked by the hand of the guilty person, it would begin to crow. Every servant had undergone the ordeal and still the cock was silent, but Napier easily found the thief. He had covered the cock's back with soot, indistinguishable in the dark, especially on black feathers. The guilty man had not dared to stroke it, so his hand was the only clean one.

Napier was annoyed by pigeons, not the wild "cushies" (wood-pigeons) or the rock-pigeons, but the "domestic doos", kept by his neighbours in dove-cots, to ensure a supply of meat for the winter. His neighbours' doos were feeding on his crops, so he complained that unless the nuisance was stopped, he would impound them. His neighbours laughed at this threat and told him to use his magic if he could.

The next morning all the ground near Merchiston was strewn with helpless doos, which Napier collected and impounded as he had threatened. He did not reveal his diabolic trick. The doos were all hopelessly drunk on grain saturated with brandy.

Michael Scott, who flourished centuries before Napier, in a period just as superstitious, had studied alchemy abroad, and was reputed to be in league with the devil. He had three attendant imps, Prig, Prim and Pricker. Acting on the old adage, "Satan still doth mischief find for idle hands to do," he was continually looking for tasks for these little devils, to prevent them from tormenting him. Parents with lively young children will sympathise with Michael. Amongst other little 'bob-a-jobs' which they did, was the splitting of the Eildon Hills in three. The Romans in their great camps at Newstead, and on the Eildon Hills, must have had remarkable second sight when, in the second century, A.D., they named the hill Trimontium, about a thousand years before Prig, Prim and

E

Pricker emerged from Hades. A great dam on the Tweed, built long after Scott's day, and in ruins in the 15th century, was still pointed out as the work of these mischievous lads.

One devilish task defied Michael Scott and his imps, as it also defied Napier of Merchiston and Black Duncan of the Cowl, 1st Laird of Glenorchy (which he stole from the clan Gregor.) They could not make ropes of sand. Many places in Scotland, notably the Culbins, are pointed out as the scene of their vain attempts to do this. Pity no one suggested glass-fibre to them.

The Eildons themselves are haunted. There, one may see druidical circles, supposed to have been devoted at one time to human sacrifice, and certainly the scene, as most of these places were, of sabbatical meetings where witches gathered: "Ringwoodie Hags wad spean a foal" and "Maidens" (i.e. Bob Mahoun's luscious young things who always sat at his side). "Cutty Sark", in Tam o' Shanter, was one of these Go-go girls.

Orgies were enacted by moonlight, compared with which the Hell-fire Clubs of the 18th century were mere Bands of Hope. The meetings were convened by the Devil giving out his "Keerie," a weird call which carried for miles over hill and dale. The witches then came flying in, mounted on creepie-stools, brooms, sieves, ragwort, hogweed, hemlock. Their first pleasant duty was to perform the "Osculum Infame" which consisted simply in each in turn kissing Bob's posterior, or to avoid the Latin derivative, his Erse, Arce (soft c) or Airss. Should the meeting be honoured by Royalty in the shape of the Queen of the Fairies (a feminine divinity in that unenlightened age) this ceremony was called "Kyssyng the Quene of Elphinis Airss."

These preliminaries over, the "hoppringles" began. These were primordial ring-a-ring-a-roses, performed in pagan times by Celtic peoples within their sacred groves or, where trees could not be induced to grow, in "corthies", roofless circular houses of dry stone rather like brochs. A Gaelic proverb still commemorates them: "There is no roof in the house of mocking."

The music was supplied by the devil himself (as in Alloway Kirk), usually on the pipes but often on other instruments. "The devil has all the best tunes" complained John Wesley. He certainly had some good ones, and words to match. Here are a few of the titles. "Tinkletum-Tankletum," "The Silly Bit Chicken," "Push the Jorum," "Kittle me Nakit Wantonlie," "Johne cum kiss me noo," "O, who is at my window, who, who?" "Pretty weil begann, man." "John Andersonne my Jo." "Kilt thy coat, Maggie." "Jenny drinks na water," "Bonnie Jean maks meikle o' me," "The Lass o Glasgowe," "Kettie Bairdie," "Pitt on your shirt on Monday."

Auld Nick now led the dance, his partner being the "Maiden." All the others joined in, doing a Conga, often as many as seven score taking part, as at North Berwick. Should the moon be obscured, or the path difficult, Auld Nick stuck a lighted candle up his Airss, unlighted end first, and led the way. Decorum demands that I do not give the details of this sexual orgy other than to quote four lines:

They'd houghmagandie a' the nicht
Like gaislins in a gaggle;
Bob gamfled left and gamfled richt
And aye played wiggle-waggle.

Of course, as the old truism has it, "Merry nichts mak sad mornins" and the history of Lowland Scotland is stained for nearly two centuries with atrocious crimes against deluded or sex-crazed women, with a minority of men. Most of these witch-burnings, duckings, prickings, were simply the result of parish or local accusation of "maleficium" or evil-doing, directed against one or two unpopular old women, who perhaps got a kick out of being associated with the devil. For quite trifling misdemeanours they were accused. Often for no other cause than expressing a wish that the "Deil wad blaw her blind, or tak a bite oot o' her."

But shamefully, larger witch-hunts, set going by James VI and persons of power, accounted for mass-burnings. There always had to be pogroms going on. If not against the Jews, then gipsies, or Templars, or wild, wild Hielandmen, or heretics of some sort. The witches were an easy prey. Scarcely a parish was without a witch-burning. Some were notorious. In the East Merse of Berwickshire every village was famous for something: Chirnside for bourtrees, bees and bairns, and Edincraw or Auchencraw, a mile or two off, was a hamlet populated almost entirely by wizards and witches, who threatened evil to all and sundry. The local proverb says,

"Ye'll get mair for your ill than for your guid, like the witches o' Edincraw;" the meaning being that threats will be more remunerative than kind words. But the Edincraw followers of Auld Nick deserved all they got, as this old ballad tells. Suspected persons were usually subjected to ducking. If they sank they were innocent, if they floated, guilty; of some it was said, they were neither so sinful as to float, nor so holy as to sink. But no such trial was given to the Edincraw witches.

> There's witches and warlocks in Edincraw
> Wha neither fear God nor regard the law;
> They've libbet a man as I heard tell,
> For whilk they'll a' be sent to Hell;
> In a barrel of feathers they stappit his heid
> And guddled the body till he be deid,
> Then into the fire his bollocks they threw;
> Deil ride the stang on the ill-deedit crew
> Till a' their buttocks be reid and sair
> And then we'll burn them ilka hair
> Upon the tap o' Sheelupdykes Hill
> Wi' barrels o' tar and gie them their fill
> O' the lowe and the reek and send them hame
> To scouther for ever in Hell's blue flame.

This area seems to have been very subject to devils, hobgoblins and Will-o-the-Wisps or Spunkies, probably because there were so many bogs and pieces of heathery wasteland interspersed with fertile fields. A demon named Droedan haunted the heaths. It may be that he was a relic of the Druids for this verse shows that he was vanquished for a time by a worthy opponent, named Billy, perhaps a local priest.

> "Billy wi' a kent sae stoot
> Turned grisly Droedan oot;
> Droedan leuch and lowpt awa
> And vanished in a babbanqua." (quaking bog.)

Up to a century ago folk returning late through haunted regions, like the Billie Mire, used to "whistle to bear their courage up" with this couplet:

"We'll a' gang thegither like the folk o' the Sheils
Defying the bogles, the ghaists and the deils."

During the "Killing Times" (the reign of Charles II), the Covenanters were persecuted by dragoons, led by prominent men, who favoured the Government policy of enforcing attendance at the Established Church. These "Men of Blood" were led by Graham of Claverhouse, or Bloody Claver'se as he was called. To meet them face to face one has only to read "Wandering Willie's Tale" by Scott. There they are depicted in Hell. Grierson of Lag (whom Scott disguised under the name Redgauntlet) was of a branch of the clan Gregor who had come south: he was one of the Devil's familiars. So also were Middleton, Rothes, Lauderdale, Dalziel, Earlshall, Bonshaw, Douglas, Bluidy Mackenzie and Laurie.

The Covenanters, living in fear of sudden death, and seeking the wilderness of the Galloway and Ayrshire Hills, were often confronted by the Devil, or by an apparition resembling him. Balfour of Burleigh, one of the murderers of Archbishop Sharp, mistook Henry Morton for the foul fiend, in Scott's Old Mortality. It was said that Claverhouse's black steed, which could gallop along a hillside as steep as a roof, was a present from the Devil. Many a Whig loaded his musket with silver bullets under the belief that the Devil had made Claverhouse lead-proof. They actually claimed they had seen the lead shot rebounding from his buff coat.

Probably the last serious attempt to present the Devil was made by James Hogg in his novel "Confessions of a Justified Sinner", a psychological study of obsession which Hogg placed in the early 18th century, when Auld Nick was fast becoming a figment of the imagination.

But even as an imagined spirit of evil he could still make trouble.

The minister of East Anstruther towards the end of the 17th century was a Mr Thomson. His father, a strong Covenanter, had objected to his son's appointment to an established church, even as far away from trouble as Fife, and this may have preyed on Thomson's mind, although he also had domestic troubles.

One evening he had gone out visiting in West Anstruther, and was returning late. The Dreel Burn is the boundary between the two burghs. To reach home he had to cross the bridge over the burn. As was the custom, a servant maid carrying a lantern went before him to light the way. As they were crossing the bridge, so she reported later, a large black dog came between them from the direction of the churchyard. She was so afraid of this apparition that she dropped the lantern. However, she saw the minister home to the manse, but the next morning he was absent. He was later found drowned in the Dreel Burn. Everyone believed that the Devil had claimed him for deserting the cause of the Covenant, and disobeying his father.

The devil was so often called upon to do an ill-deed that he must have had a busy time. A minister in Dumfries was walking to officiate at a funeral when he met an Irishman driving a flock of geese. He ran here and there, trying to keep them in marching order, but with little success so he cried out, "The divil choke the boggers."

A little farther along the road, outside a farmyard, the minister came on a young man driving a herd of swine, who were also hard to guide. He cried out,

"The devil tak them." The minister went up to him and said, "Your friend the devil will be along in a minute. He's busy down the road choking some geese for an Irish gentleman."

For a long time, humanity has given up belief in supernatural devils but still believes firmly, with every cause, in human devils.

An old minister was preaching on the subject of miracles in a Dundee church. He was constantly interrupted by a gang of youths in the gallery who were noisily eating pea-nuts and tossing the shells upon the bald heads of venerable members in the pews below. At last his patience ran out. He pointed to the offenders and exclaimed; "I'm no, like my Maister, able to perform miracles, but I'm a grand hand at castin' oot devils." This threat secured silence.

THE HEREAFTER

The two important questions about life remain to be answered: where did it come from; and where does it go to? We do not seem to have got any further forward than the old Anglian poet who compared earth to a great hall, warm and hospitable in a long winter's night: man's soul is like a sparrow that flies in at a window, stays for a time, and flies out by another window into the vast darkness.

On a tombstone at Stirling a similar idea, likening a man's life to a visit to an inn on a winter's day, is put into a pithy rhyme.

> Some only breakfast and away,
> Others to dinner stay and are full fed,
> The oldest man but sups and goes to bed.

But none of this provides an answer to either question, particularly to the second, which is the subject of this chapter: where does man's spirit go to?

It may well be asked, what has Scotland to do in particular with the hereafter, that elusive region of spirits, apparitions; and arguments which are never likely to be satisfactorily ended?

Well, as it happens, Scotland is uniquely placed for dealing with this problem, principally because the Scots, though a very mixed race, have a strong framework of Celtic peoples supporting them. No less than three branches of Celts were long established in Scotland; the Picts, Britons and Gaels. They have absorbed invasions of Germanic peoples but have not lost their original beliefs in that nebulous spirit world; the Danes, Norse and Angles also had a mythology to contribute to Scottish belief in the other invisible existence.

To mediaeval people all over Christendom there was never any doubt about the awful reality of the hereafter. Dante, in his three great works, gave a very graphic and exact picture of Purgatory, Heaven and Hell, not sparing to name those who had gone there. The Celtic idea of the after-life was totally different from this.

But the centuries passed and the age of disbelief came, when philosophers discredited a future existence, or a world of the spirit. This atheism, or agnosticism, worried the churchmen and sent them searching in all directions for proof of a hereafter or a spirit world. This led grave and learned men like Dr Samuel Johnson and many others to give credit to ghost stories, tales of second sight and apparitions. They haunted Cock Lane, and sat up to see ghosts in London churchyards, but the most fruitful area for their investigations proved to be Scotland, especially the Highlands where no-one doubted the powers of seers, or the return of wraiths from the hereafter.

Efforts were made by sceptics, Scots as well as English, to ridicule and discredit these reports. In many cases the claims of the spirit-world were shown to be false and even ludicrous, but quite a number were so well authenticated that they could not be disputed.

I have collected a large number of these stories and reports, and I shall write them fairly, leaving the reader to laugh or suspend disbelief, according to the evidence. I have also included some remarkable instances of immortality, i.e. persons who have far surpassed the ordinary span of life and have, so to speak, over-stayed their leave in this world. Not one of these aged persons in Scotland comes within a long way of equalling Old Parr, the Englishman, who lived to be 152. When asked by Charles II if he had done anything remarkable, apart from living so long, he amused the Merry Monarch by confessing that a young woman had successfully brought a suit for patrimony against him, when he was over 100.

I had a distant relative named Graham who, when over 100, carried a sack of seed potatoes on his back from Carlisle to Longtown, nine miles. He was then keen on gardening, but so far as I know, did not try the grass on the other side of the matrimonial fence.

In Lasswade Kirkyard there is, or was, a peculiar gravestone erected to a Terence Dugan who was born on March 4th, 1700, and died on December 4th, 1800, aged 100 years and 9 months.

The commentator says, "Had he been born a few months earlier he would have lived during part of three centuries." But this is an error of fact, for 1700 was the last year of the 17th century, and 1800 the last year of the 18th century, so all that Terence should have done to qualify for a man of three centuries was to have lived for another four weeks, until 1st January 1801. Still, it was a "close-run thing."

71

But a peculiarly long-lived family were the Grays, who had no other great achievements. Betty Gray lived to be 108 and, as her father had died before she went to school, she survived him by over a century. Her father had had a son much earlier, who died young, so Betty could truthfully say that her brother had died 128 years before. Her mother was 96, and her sisters 94 and 96, at their deaths.

In my hiking days, about fifty years ago, I found a very good camping-site above the Liddesdale road, on a little grassy plateau by a rill that runs below Ettleton Kirkyard. There was a sheltering wood close by. We explored the ancient kirkyard, which had some very strange memorials: one to a man murdered, or shot in a duel; but the one that had to do with extreme old age was to Margaret Wylie, who died aged 113. It is related by Robert Chambers in "Picture of Scotland" that this woman was "tedding" hay in that very field, where, as a "gilpy" lassie, a century before to the very day, she had been engaged on the same task.

A very violent man, a "Bloody Bell," is commemorated by a red sandstone memorial, now probably swallowed up in Solway quicksands at Redkirk, Gretna. It is strange that he survived so long, but there is no reason to doubt it for his memorial stated.

> Here lieth Jon Bell who died in ye yhere
> MDX and of his age CXXX yheres.

followed by ten lines enumerating this stark mosstrooper's atrocities. The good die young.

The reputedly oldest man in Scotland died, aged 132, at the beginning of the 19th century. He was John Gordon, of Turriff, in North-West Aberdeenshire. There is no reason to question the truth about his great age, but less credible is a tale told about a young English visitor to the town, who had been informed by the landlady of the inn where to find the 'oldest man in Aberdeenshire, aye, and in the world.'

He went to the cottage where Gordon lived and saw an old man knitting socks at the door. "Can you see to knit at the age of 132?" "I'm only 73. It's my grandfather you're seeking."

Round the corner of the cottage, the visitor came upon a very old whitehaired man, dull of hearing, but it turned out that this was only a centenarian, and not yet John Gordon, who was ultimately found digging potatoes in the kailyard. "Aye, it's a God's mercy I'm still able to dae a bit wark, for the laddies, puir things, are gey far through."

Another strange tale of survivors concerns a grave scandal of the late 18th century.

Henry Dundas of Arniston was one of a distinguished Lothians family. When a young man of 23, a penniless advocate, he married Elizabeth Rennie, 15, the heiress to the Melville estates, who was worth about £100,000. Dundas, who kept a note of every Scots voter (and his ambitious sons and nephews), used to boast that he carried every Scottish M.P. in his pocket, in Pitt's interest. Corruption has never gone deeper. Anyway, his parliamentary business kept him from his wife and family for long periods, and his wife got weary of it. She eloped with Captain Faukener when she was 28, in 1778. Sir Alexander Dick wrote "Lord Advocate divorced last week from his *criminal* wife and she married soon after to the man who caused it, a vile scandalous affair on her part and his who is saddled with her and will probably soon suffer by her." 'She played her cards very ill' was the most charitable view. She was never heard of again. She was dead in the eyes of her husband, the law and the world. . . .

60 years later her great-grandson Sir Robert Dundas of Arniston was turning over the estate accounts when he noticed a small annuity paid to a Mrs Faukener. He asked if she was a family servant, and was told that she was his great-grandmother, who had brought the title and Castle of Melville and £100,000 into the family, and was living near Land's End where she continued to live as far away as possible from her hated native land, until she was nearly 98.

> Betty's gane frae Melville Castle
> Hooted, spurned by a'.
> Gey glad to gie them a' "Fareweel";
> And then ootlived them a'.

Many of these claims to longevity are founded on weak evidence, as compulsory registration did not begin until the middle of the 19th century. Parish registers, however, are very reliable.

I now come to some very strange ways of achieving immortality, but first I ought to make a passing comment on what our immortal bard himself had to say on the subject. "One thing frightens me much. That we are to live for ever seems too good to be true." Perhaps it would have frightened him more had he foreseen what volleys the "Awkward Squads" were to fire over his grave for ever and ever. It is strange that he jokingly wrote that there might come a day when his birthday would be kept as a national festival.

Those who have been certified dead can be said to have entered the hereafter officially. If they return, as some few of them do, it is against all the rules of the game.

Maggie Dickson of Musselburgh was one of these. Her husband had been absent for a year, and was due to return when Maggie had just given birth to a child. To avoid a quarrel, she murdered the child, and was condemned to be hanged in Edinburgh. Sentence was carried out. Her friends cut her down and put her in a cart, but, being in no hurry, they stopped at Peffermill to have a few drinks. When they came out of the pub, Maggie was sitting up in her rude hearse, grumbling at being left out of the party, and at the roughness of the road.

Her brief sojourn in the hereafter did not redeem her, for despite a moral sermon preached at her in the kirk for the encouragement of the "Honest Toon" generally, she continued to sin until she entered the hereafter for the second and final time.

I had a great friend who for over half a century kept before him a plaque from the War Office, commemorating his death on the battlefield in Flanders in 1914. There cannot be very many who, like Mark Twain, have had to tell their friends that the report of their departure into the hereafter has been "grossly exaggerated."

Frances-Theresa Stuart, Duchess of Lennox, of East Lothian, was the handsomest woman in the court of Charles II. Naturally she won his very susceptible heart and he wished to divorce his queen and marry her, but this was prevented by her marriage to another. Nevertheless the Merry Monarch made

73

this lovely lady immortal by having her struck on the coinage to represent Britannia. There she sits forever, tall, majestic, "in a voluptuous completeness of feature and person." We have never since on our coinage approached this majestic divinity.

Ministers of the gospel were serious and truth-telling men whose testimony could not be lightly brushed aside. Such a man was Robert Kirke, the minister of Aberfoyle. He was, like most Celts, a firm believer in the "Light Infantry of Satan."

He was walking upon the Fairy Mound, a little knoll to the west of his manse (thinking perhaps of the remarkable book, "The Secret Commonwealth" which he had recently written on the fairy world), when he sank down in a swoon. He was taken up for dead and was buried. Shortly afterwards he appeared in a dream to a near relative and informed him to let it be known that he was not dead, but was in fairyland, and that when his child was baptised he would appear. If a knife were thrown over his head he would return to earth.

This dream was repeated. When the baptismal day arrived, the party were seated at table; the figure of Robert Kirke entered, but his relative neglected to throw the knife over him so he went out by another door, never to re-appear.

His book was printed in Edinburgh in 1815. Sir Walter Scott gives all these particulars in the notes to "Rob Roy."

There are several instances of persons who have been abducted into the fairy hereafter. These are fictional, as in the case of Bonny Kilmeny and Tamlane, well-known in Border lore. But Thomas Learmonth of Ercildoune (Earlston) swore that he had lodged in fairyland for seven years, and had been endowed with the power of poetic speech by the Fairy Queen; and who are we to dispute this, in the face of his remarkable poetic productions.

I was with a party of teachers and camping-pupils one summer evening at sunset on the Fairy Mound at Aberfoyle. No bird sang, nor ever sings, in that wood. Standing in the centre of the circle of Scots pines that crown the hill, one could easily confuse this world and the hereafter of the Secret Commonwealth.

This belief, in the power of the fairies to carry people off, persisted well into modern times. It was customary near Scots villages, Highland and Lowland alike, to leave a piece of land uncultivated. This was named the "Gudeman's Croft," in deference to the Devil and his imps: to mention their names near this ground was to risk instant immortality, in a fairy hereafter, which was under the rule of Hell and from which, according to the legend, a human soul had to be delivered to the Devil every seven years by way of rent.

People were never quite sure how they would go into the hereafter. An old lady in the Borders seemed to think that it entailed an aerial flight, such as the Rev. Robert Kirke describes in the "Secret Commonwealth". As she drew near her end in a terrible night of thunder and lightening she glanced fearfully through the window and muttered to her friends, "Michty me, whit a nicht to be fleein' through the air."

All through the centuries there have been groups of zealots who have expected to be translated into the hereafter without experiencing death. Off the High Street of Edinburgh, near where the Netherbow Port once stood, is the World's End Close, named after a band of enthusiasts who daily expected the Millenium.

R. L. Stevenson has written about a similar band of Westland Covenanters who encamped for a time on the north side of the Pentland Hills, waiting to see

Auld Reekie go up in smoke like Sodom and Gomorrah. Their hopes must have been raised briefly every evening for, when suppers were being prepared, a few thousand lums sent up reek to heaven. But this was a phenomenon well-known for miles around; across in Fife an old laird used to time his own supper by watching for the smoke signals from across the Forth. The Covenanters eventually went home to await the Millenium in a more comfortable place than the Pentlands in winter.

The Buchanites was another religious body of doom-watchers. They followed Mother Buchan in awaiting a special booking for a flight into the hereafter. They built a platform on a hillside in Galloway, so that they could be more easily airborne. On the prophesied day, they crowded on to it, but owing to a structural weakness they were precipitated hugger-mugger to Mother Earth. But Mother Buchan, her faith unshattered, merely deferred the Day of Judgment, and entered the hereafter by the common door. Robert Burns, in a letter of August 1784, gives an account of this strange sect.

David Hume, the agnostic philosopher, had a very solid cylindrical mausoleum built for himself in the New Calton. It is a prominent feature today, though grimy with railway smoke. A very substantial door with a massive lock protected him from the attentions of "resurrectionists" for these ghouls were stirring long before Burke and Hare. After the interment the door was locked. A cynical gentleman asked the mason how he expected Hume to get out at the Judgment Day to meet Gabriel and answer for his short-comings. To this the mason replied, with a wry smile, "O, I've ta'en guid care o' that. I've slippit the key under the door. He can please himsel whether he comes oot or bides in."

A prosperous Dumfries merchant, an acknowledged atheist, got a mausoleum built to rival that of Burns. He supervised the construction and rather annoyed the clerk of works with his criticisms. The beadle of a neighbouring kirk came to see the edifice.
"A braw vault, is it no?" said the merchant. Then scoffingly added, "It's that strong it'll tak us a' oor time to rise through the roof at the Judgment Day."
"Ne'er fash your thoomb about that," replied the beadle. "They'll just ding oot the erse o't and let ye a' fa' through."

At Durisdeer away up in the Lowther Hills, is the tomb of the Queensberry family. Here is to be seen a very quaint and ornate sepulchre. The Duke of Queensberry in the splendour of top-boots, long surtout with ample buttons and all the Carolean wig-maker's craft piled up, is bending solicitously over his Duchess who is arrayed in the supernumerary fal-de-rals of the period. Well might he appear a little worried about her health, for she pre-deceased him by a few years. There they lie in the marble hereafter, like a pair of brontosauri fossilised in limestone.
Some persons before going into the hereafter decided to bid farewell to their friends and acquaintances on earth, often to their great surprise and dismay.
When the Earl of Balcarres was imprisoned in Edinburgh Castle, the ghost of James Graham of Claverhouse (Bonnie Dundee) appeared to him in his cell. Graham had a ghastly face, blood-bespattered but smiling, his dark eyes fixed piercingly on Balcarres. He did not speak and soon vanished. It was some days later that Balcarres got to hear of Graham's death at Killiecrankie, on the very hour of his appearance in the Castle.

A smile was on his visage
For within his dying ear
Pealed the joyful note of triumph
And the clansmen's clamorous cheer.

Dr Hibbert, to whom I refer later, rather illogically tried to explain this by suggesting Balcarres suffered from delusions because he was in poor health at the time of his captivity.

A tippler was taking a short cut across the kirkyard of a northern parish when he fell into a new-dug grave and did not awake until the trumpet of a rag-and-bone merchant roused him. He scrambled out and surveying the quiet graveyard, himself the only soul stirring, exclaimed, "Gabriel's horn tootin for the Day o' Doom; a gey puir turnoot for Aberchirder."

The majority of Christian Scots looked forward to the resurrection, more in hope than in certainty, but for two centuries the Resurrectionist Movement was of quite a different nature. This was grave-robbing, "one of the foulest blots on Scottish civilisation," in the words of George MacGregor, a Glasgow journalist who wrote the History of the Resurrectionists, which culminated in the notorious mass murders by Burke and Hare in Edinburgh a century and a half ago.

It is not easy to find humour in the callous adventures of these ghouls, whether murderers or merely robbers, but there is one true tale of these hellish cantrips which alleviates the horror of the midnight hour, when "denizens of nether hell breathed the free air of earth" and unscrupulous merchants of human carrion, armed with shovels and lanterns, crept about their trade and made the hereafter an unholy abode furnished with scalpels and dissecting tables.

Before descending to the bathos of my tale of ongoings in Auld Reekie in the hey-day of the Ressurectionists, I think it is worth mentioning, to show the horror in which the dissection of humans was held, that Pope Benedict XII uttered a malediction on hearing of the desire by the dying King Robert Bruce that his heart should be cut from his body and taken to Jerusalem by Douglas. It is a pity the Pope's curse was not listened to, for the useless death of Douglas was a disaster for Scotland, as events soon proved.

There were three worthies in Edinburgh who plied the body-snatching trade and were pre-eminent in their profession. One was Merrylees, nicknamed Merry-Andrew; he was very tall, thin and gaunt, with a pale face and ogre's jaws. His clothes hung about him, rather than on him. His walk was springy and his face was lively with horrid contortions. The second of the trio of ghouls was known as the "Spune"; his real name not of consequence. He looked like a broken-down parson, he was feeble-minded, but as grave and dignified as the most eminent professor of medicine. The third partner was Mowatt, known as the "Moudiewart," or mole. He had been a plasterer but had left that messy business for a more profitable one, not forgetting to bring his trowel. "I, said the owl, with my little trowel, I'll dig his grave." The several episodes in their "career open to the talons" may be read in George Macgregor's 'Burke and Hare', but this one may serve to amuse.

Merrylees had cheated his partners of ten shillings, so they waited their chance of revenge. It came at last, they thought, when Merrylees' sister died at Penicuik.

Moudiewart and the Spune decided to lift the deceased, and, so to speak, kill two birds with one stone. They hired a donkey and cart and, arriving at Penicuik Kirkyard between twelve and one, began to howk. As they got the body out they heard an unearthly howl and saw a white-robed figure floating towards them with outstreched arms. They fled to the donkey-cart and made for Edinburgh. The "ghost" was Merrylees himself, who had heard from the owner of the donkey-cart of their plan. Remarking (wittily in the circumstances) "The 'Spune' shall lack its porridge and Merry-Andrew shall live on the fruit of the earth," he shouldered his sister and sprang forward so fast that he overtook the pair in the donkey-cart, who abandoned the quadruped as being too slow, and showed how fast bipeds could go. Merrylees put the cart to good use, and soon collected the reward of his fraternal affection in Surgeons' Square.

Dr John Abercrombie, surgeon to Queen Victoria, died suddenly one forenoon in 1844 at York Place, Edinburgh, as he was about to enter his carriage. That very same day, at Blairlogie, Perthshire, a friend of the family, a lady from Jamaica, had had a strange dream. She saw the whole Abercrombie family, in white, dancing a solemn funeral dance, or pavane, to slow music. Shortly after, a servant came running from the garden to tell her that Dr Abercrombie, pale-faced and shaking his head, was leaning against a wall as she walked by the house. The lady wrote to Edinburgh to inquire of the doctor's health, the letter taking two days to go. Her fears were confirmed by the reply, but she could get no rational explanation for the double message from the hereafter.

A stranger case of a person apparently returning from the hereafter took place in Edinburgh in the 18th century. The London coach pulled in at Whitehorse Close near Holyroodhouse and the usual crowd of porters and friends met it. As a gentleman alighted, he was approached by his former butler, John ——, who greeted him warmly. When asked how he did, the butler said his affairs were in a pretty low state. The gentleman asked if he could go with him to his house which lay in rather a poor quarter. On arriving there and knocking at the door, the butler's wife, whom the gentleman knew of old, answered and invited him in. On turning round to allow the butler to enter, he found to his astonishment that he had vanished. His surprise was turned to shock when the lady informed him that her husband had died three years before.

In 1824 Dr Hibbert of Edinburgh published a learned book entitled "The Philosophy of Apparitions," in which he went to some length to explain away all ghosts and apparitions as figments of the mind. But, in the interests of truth, he is forced to end his book with the following true tale which came to him from a manuscript of Dr Archibald Pitcairn (1651-1713) founder of the famous Edinburgh School of Medicine. I give it exactly as it is written. Hibbert calls it "one of the most curious ghost stories I have ever seen."

"Robert Lindsay, grandchild, or great grandchild, to Sir David Lindsay of ye Month, Lyon King at Arms, etc. being intimate condisciple (fellow-student) with A.P. (Arch. Pitcairn) they bargained, anno 1671, that whoever dyed first should give account of his condition if possible. It happened that he dyed about the end of 1675 while A.P. was at Paris; and the very night of his death A.P. dreamed that he was at Edinburgh, where Lindsay attacked him thus:— "Archie," said he, "perhaps ye heard I'm dead?"—"No, Roben."—"Aye, but they burie my body in the Greyfryers. I am alive though in a place whereof the pleasures cannot be exprest in Scotch, Greek or Latine. I have come with a well-sailing small ship to Leith Road, to carry you thither."—"Roben, I'll go with you, but wait till I go to Fife and East-Lothian and take leave of my parents."—"Archie, I have but the allowance of one tide. Farewell, I'll come for you at another time."

Since which time A.P. never slept at night without dreaming that Lindsay told him he was alive. And having a dangerous sickness, anno 1694, he was told by Roben that he was delayed for a time, and that it was properly his task to carry him off, but was discharged (forbidden) to tell when."

Trials of long-dead corpses was a macabre mockery which James VI held upon those who had offended him and had eluded justice by slipping into the hereafter. Logan of Restalrig's corpse was subjected to this, after his failure to provide James with treasure supposed to have been buried at Fast Castle on the cliffs of Berwickshire.

In England Cromwell's corpse was brought back to face those who would not have dared to bend their brows on him in his lifetime.

Apparitions thin and fast come crowding upon us.

The minister of Borthwick was awakened every morning at the same early hour by three knocks on his bedroom door. If he did not answer (and he never did), the knocks came to the head of his bed. He ignored them, and they, or it, went away to return every morning at the same time. He did not choose to light a candle to see what spectre was disturbing him.

The house of the notorious Major Weir (who, with his magic stick and his sister, was burned at Greenside beside the Calton Hill in Edinburgh), was haunted for long after his death. This house was in the Bow. People passing at night used to report that it was full of lights and noises of revelry with the most hideous screeches mingled through it. Years after this satanic soiree had been dispersed, nobody would take the house, even when offered free of rent. At last a cobbler and his wife, despite warnings, moved in. The first night they had scarce got to bed when an apparition in the shape of a calf came out of the chimney-place, walked to their bed and gazed fixedly at them.

They flitted hurriedly at daybreak, never to return.

At the old Edinburgh mansion-house of Wrighthouses which was cleared to make way for Gillespie's Hospital, there was a negro servant called Black Tom. He was constantly haunted by the ghost of a lovely young lady carrying an infant. People laughed at his hallucinations, but their mocking was turned to gasps of horror, when during renovation, the hearthstone of his room was lifted to reveal the skeletons of a young woman and an infant which had lain there for generations. The lady had been beheaded.

Strathmore Castle, the childhood home of the Queen Mother was long haunted by a horrific spectre known as Earl Beardie. Like the Icelandic ghosts, this one did not stop at mere haunting, but resorted to such crude violence as strangling and chopping etc. if all reports are true. A secret room was where he holed out.

Scots had so little faith in their earthly future, or were so canny, that they often qualified any plans with the phrase "if I'm spared." An old lady was admiring the neatly-kept churchyard and remarked to her friend, "Eh, I'd like fine to be buried here some day, if I'm spared."

Another, on a weekly tea-taking at her friend's house, bade farewell with these words, "Weel, good-bye, Jenny, and I'll be along next Friday at four, if I'm spared." To which Jenny replied a little acidly, "And if ye're no spared, Teeny, I'll no expect ye."

A very formal lady of the old school had a little maid whom she trained in all the etiquette of small-town society. One sad morning little Susan knocked at her mistress's door to bring her a cup of tea, to find the old lady had passed away during the night. She dressed herself in coat and hat and crossed over to her mistress's friend to inform her of the sad news.
She knocked politely and when the lady appeared she curtseyed and announced "Miss Stark's compliments, ma'am, and she dee'd this morning afore seven o'clock."

We come now to much more serious tales of malicious and dangerous ghosts.
In Selkirk, long ago, a soutar, or shoemaker, as was the custom, began working very early on a winter morning. A stranger knocked at the door and ordered a pair of shoes which he said he would call for at a later day. He went away before cock-crow.
A few days later he came at the same early hour, paid for the shoes and took them away. Something strange in the customer's appearance induced the soutar to follow him. He went into the kirkyard and disappeared into a grave which the soutar marked by sticking his awl into it.
Summoning a company of fellow tradesmen the soutar returned. They opened the grave and discovered the new-made shoes on the coffin. The soutar took the shoes and went back with them to his shop. Next day, before dawn, as he was working, the zombie entered, his face transfigured with rage.
"You've stolen what I paid for. Ye hae made me a warld's wunner but I'll sune mak ye a greater."
He dragged the wretch to the kirkyard, where his body was later found on the desecrated grave, torn limb from limb.

The "zombie" objected strongly to being cheated, but another ghost who had been starved to death, was quite violent too.
Lady Jardine of Applegarth in Dumfriesshire was a miser. She used to sit in rags by the banks of the Annan and carry people over pick-a-back for a halfpenny.
A miller named Porteous was suspected of having set fire to his mill and was confined to the dungeons of Spedlins Tower, owned by Sir Alexander Jardine of Applegarth. Sir Alexander was called to Edinburgh and left the miller in charge of his miserly lady. To make matters worse it was only when he reached Edinburgh that Jardine realised he had taken away the keys of the dungeon. He sent a courier back, but in the interval Porteous had died of hunger. It is not known whether Lady Jardine ignored his cries for food. It seems likely.
The ghost of Porteous now began to haunt the Jardines, so a number of ministers were assembled to exorcise the ghost. They did this by chaining a large bible to the gate of the dungeon, which effectively kept the spirit inside, where, however, it incessantly cried, "Let me oot. Let me oot. I'm deein' o' hunger."
After putting up with this for years the Jardines built a new house across the

river and forgot about the ghost. But the Bible was sent away to Edinburgh to be rebound in calf-skin and that night the ghost of Porteous got out, crossed the river without difficulty, and entered the new house where it tumbled the furniture about, and hauled Sir Alexander and his lady out of bed. A messenger was sent to get the Bible back as soon as possible, without bothering about the binding. It was Porteous that had to be bound. The Bible is still to be seen, but the ghost has ceased from troubling, and the Jardines are at rest.

Another homicidal ghost used to haunt the ruins of Kilchrist church at Beauly. One evening a little Highland tailor, who travelled about making up suits, came into the inn at Beauly. In the course of talk, he boasted that he cared very little about ghosts. He was dared to go to the ruin and rough-stitch a suit of clothes which he had already cut out. A bet was made that he would get a suit-length when he returned, so with this in mind, he set out under the full moon.

He sat cross-legged on a flat tomb and began on the breeches. Before long, a grisly skeletal leg emerged from the ground and a hollow voice said, "Do you see this leg?" to which he replied (in Gaelic) "That I see, this I sew."

In turn another leg appeared, then two arms, to all of which he responded in the same words. Finally as he drew the last stitch on the jacket a skull came up and a battle-axe. He ran for the doorway as the dry bones connected. Luckily he was not tall and the axe crashed into the lintel just above his head. He got back to collect his web but vowed never to revisit Kilchrist.

Longformacus is an isolated ideal village among the Lammermoor Hills. It used to be difficult to reach because of long hilly roads to it. Early in the 19th century the village blacksmith was Neil, an uncouth man who didn't respect other people's rights. He had a sister at Swinton, a village about ten miles off. She had never been on good terms with Neil, nor had anybody else, but he attended her funeral and returned home via a dark wooded road. As he related later, in the darkness, a great "flaff" of light struck him and shocked him so much that he had difficulty in reaching home. He never recovered, dying some months later. His son, a man of similar temper, was returning from a distant visit not long after and had to pass the dreary place where his father had seen the "flaff". But as he did not arrive home a search was made and his body was found; his underwear was over his clothes, as if the demon had stripped him and put his clothes back in reverse. These two stories are true, as I verified from old Longformacians nearly fifty years ago.

Every town has its visitors from the hereafter, as had many country districts. Only two miles from where the Neils met their end is a place called Foulfordlee where a midnight coach drawn by spectral horses used to appear.

In Leith the "Twelve o'clock Coach" was sometimes heard and less frequently seen. There was also a Green Lady, a Fairy Drummer Boy on the Calton Hill (then South Leith Common) and a horror called Shellycoat, who passed his name on to the bailiff's men, who were equally to be avoided.

What folk would have done without the hereafter it is hard to imagine. The minister found it a help to keep his flock in order. A young minister was given the advice, "Keep them weel ower the mooth o' Hell." "A Kirk withoot a Hell is no worth a damned docken," was another opinion.

A minister of the old Hell-fire brigade told his congregation, looking for comfort in the hereafter;

"When ye're a' doon there scoutherin' in brimstone ye'll maybe cry, 'O, Lord, hae mercy. We didna ken aboot your wrath.' And the Lord in his infinite mercy will look doon on ye and say, "Ye didna ken? Weel, ye ken noo."

An old Highland lady thought she would escape, and when the minister thundered, "Yes, in that day, there will be weeping and wailing and gnashing of teeth." "But I've nae teeth," she protested. He was ready for her. "Teeth will be provided." A sort of National Hell Service.

Nobody who had been in Hell had come back to tell his congregation the real facts of that region. If only Dante had visited Scotland he could have given them all the details. He was pointed out in the streets of Florence; "Behold, the man who has visited Hell." But one or two ministers were quite well-qualified.

The candidate for a kirk was being considered. He had a very unusual degree in addition to his studies in theology. It was a B.Sc. in mining engineering. This was objected to by some of the elders, but one spoke up for him.

"He'll hae a guid working knowledge o' the lower regions, and that's mair than ye can say o' the milk and water lads."

No one doubts nowadays that man does not need to provide the hereafter with devils, tortures, burnings and hideous noises. They are here, and we would all be delighted to consign them to where they belong.

A Highlandman, "big in the body and small in the head," was haunted by a ghost night and day. He was known to all as Donald the Ghost. Donald was a very simple man and it worried him that this "doppelganger" should be always with him, sticking closer than a brother. He asked his friends what he should do to get rid of it.

"If you cross running water the ghost cannot follow you," he was told. So to make quite sure he took a passage to Baltimore. But to his annoyance the first person he met on the quayside was the ghost.

"How did you get here?" he asked angrily.

"Ach," said the ghost, "I just came round about." (i.e. via Russia, Mongolia and America.)

A psychiatrist would perhaps suggest that he made the ocean-crossing before the mast, in Donald's head.

In Edinburgh a well-known character was haunted by a horrible ghostly skeleton. His case actually engaged the attention of several doctors who were interested in the philosophy of apparitions. They decided to try an experiment and asked the poor man to come up to a room in the medical school.

"Is the ghost in this room?" asked one of the doctors.

"O aye, he's ower there in the faraway corner makin' faces at me."

The doctor winked at his colleagues and crossed over to the far corner. He planted himself squarely across it and asked the afflicted one,

"Do you see him now?"

"Hoo can I see him when you're in the way?"

Then a moment later he said, "Noo I can see him brawly. He's gotten his baney fingers on your shouthers and he's girnin' at me roond the side o' your heid."

The doctors hurriedly ended their investigations and left the room.

We now come to the obviously untrue tales of the hereafter; their name is legion.

A pawky old blether met an elder friend from one of the exclusive churches in Glasgow; let us call it Snobgate.

"Man, I had a very funny dream last night. I dreamt I was deid, and mair funnily still, I dreamt I was in Heaven. Peter conducted me through miles o' corridors, past doors where there was psalm-singing and hymn-singing coming oot.

There was a special room. No' a soond cam oot. Peter keekit through the keyhole and telt me to gang by on tiptoe.

'Wha's in there?' I asked.

'O, thae's the Snobgate U.P. folk,' says Peter wi' a grin, 'They think there's naebody here but themsels.'"

A young man belonged to a family where his father and three brothers were all ministers, who looked upon him as rather a black sheep.

One cold morning he came down rather late to breakfast to find the others had all finished and were discussing some theological point round the fireside.

"You were very late in returning last night," accused his father.

"O, before midnight. I'm over twenty, you know."

"You probably slept badly," said one brother.

"O, yes, very badly. I dreamt I was in hell."

"A fairly true forecast," said the father.

"What was it like?" said another brother.

"Much the same as here." said the prodigal.

"How so?"

"I couldn't get near the fire for ministers."

A Highlander, defying all the laws of probability, found himself at Heaven's gate. St Peter appeared.

"Name, please?"

"Angus Macdonald."

"Place of residence on earth?"

"Achnashellach."

"You're the first from there. I'm not going to admit you, I'm afraid."

"But I'm a Kirk elder, very religious, God-fearing."

"I know. It's all in your file. But no entry."

"Why not then?"

"I'm not getting up early every morning all through eternity to make porridge for one."

A Scot died and his soul sought a place to spend eternity. He tried at the Golden Gates. Peter asked his name.

"Angus MacFarlane."

"Hoots awa, man," said Peter, in a broad fishertown accent. "The place is fu' o' Macs as it is. There's nae room for a MacFarlane o' a' folk."

Angus presented himself to Lucifer at the sooty gates. The devil answered his request very blandly in Oxford English.

"I should have thought that you would have gained admittance in the other place where all your compatriots are gathered together. I'm afraid I cannot allow you entry. You Scotsmen would very soon be running the establishment and relegating me to a back seat."

82

Angus reluctantly tried Purgatory as a last resort but was again refused on the grounds that he was too well up in theology. In despair Angus looked around at the black unfriendly emptiness of space then sighed and groaned out,

"Ma Goad. This is the end o' a'thing. There's nae help for it noo. I'll just hae to gang back to Glesca."

One old Hawick lady, near her end, was asked by a neighbour to make sure, when she got to heaven, to make social calls on all her friends. She replied indignantly.

"Div ye think I'll hev naething better on my mind than to gan clatter, clatter through the streets o' Heaven seeking oot your fowk?"

The mill-workers at that time wore clogs with iron-shod soles.

Another old Hawick dame observed, with a good deal of truth:

"I've noticed, if I dinna dee in the Februar, I dinna dee a' that year."

Here lies the body
of Tammas Denholm,
If ye saw him now,
ye widna ken him.

POETS

In English there are twenty polite expressions meaning poet but about thirty impolite words for much the same thing. Scotland can quite easily outnumber the rude descriptions, but luckily most of these are in Old Scots, which only language students understand. Being a poet or makar comes under the heading of dangerous occupations.

Anyone can claim to be a poet. The common idea used to be that if you strung a rhyme together you were a poet; nowadays it is even easier; you don't need to make it rhyme. This is perhaps a better idea, for some of the rhyme masters of the past were highly ridiculous.

I don't approve of mocking McGonagall, a natural who was made the butt of sick jokes. Although born in the Cowgate of Edinburgh, he was out of his element in Scotland. In his time, and ages before, Ireland had hundreds of McGonagalls who were the newsvendors of the common folk. They travelled round the country telling their listeners in entertaining style, mixed with rhyme, all the events of the day. McGonagall did this rather well too, but his audiences were aliens.

The Scots bred enough serio-comic poets of their own, without importing Irishmen.

The historian, Ritson, a very learned but irritable man, awards a place of honour in the roll of Scots poets to Black Agnes, grand-niece of Bruce, Countess Cospatrick, for the couplet she made on the spur of the moment when she was defending Dunbar Castle against Montague, Earl of Salisbury, at a time when the Scots had lost nearly all they gained at Bannockburn. The story is a favourite in Scottish history.

Montague, copying the Roman covering shield for pioneers undermining castle-walls in a siege, had build a movable shed called a sow, under which his men could work. But Black Agnes somehow had obtained an enormous boulder which was manoeuvred into position right over Montague's shield. Just before launching her thunderbolt Agnes called to the English leader,

"Beware Montague
For farrow sall thy soo."

The boulder crashed through the roof of the shed, and the survivors fled just like little pigs from under their mother.

It is a pity that modern singers of Scots songs confine themselves to a small repertoire. There are hundreds of Scottish songs in all humours, comical, satirical, lyrical; laments and songs of merriment, which survived from long before Burns' time. He had an abundance of material to hand, apart from his own original love-songs and poems. Some poets were famous for one song only, some for merely a verse, some for a line. On extremely rare occasions a poetic father had a poet for a son. Robert Burns had high hopes that his son Robert, on whom he lavished all his love and care, would turn out a better poet than himself, but from the two songs ascribed to him, "Love" and "O, pity an auld Highland piper" (in Ross's "Songs of Scotland") he had no poetic ability, as far as one can judge.

But the Semples of Beltrees produced three generations of excellent poets, one of whom wrote the famous lament for Habbie Simson, the Town Piper of Kilbarchan, his verse form providing a model for Fergusson and Burns, while another wrote the lively 'Maggie Lauder.'

Some men, renowned for anything but poetry, tried their hand at it with disastrous results.

In Aberdeen a worthy citizen, John Moody, out of the generosity of his heart, walled-in the kirkyard at Fit o' Dee, and inscribed this ingenious rhyme on the wall.

"I, John Moody, Civis Abredonesis
Builded this Kirkyaird o' fitty, upon my ain expenses."

To this day, Aberdeen men will quote this when they pay for something themselves. "This is upon my ain expenses," as Moody said.

The Earl of Mar was not as generous as John Moody. When he built a wall around his park he had a conspicuous stone built into it on which was the warning.

"Who so loups this dike o' mine
Ten pounds Scots shall be his fine." (16/8d (83p) English money.)

John Rennie, famous architect of Westminster and London Bridges, was once, and once only, inspired to poetry. This was at Tyndrum in 1797 when he was perhaps being stung by midges or soaked in rain.

"Barren are Caledonia's hills
Infertile are her plains
Bare-legged are her brawney nymphs
Bare-arsed are her swains."

85

In these stern lines we can see a foreshadow of his strong, graceful, but unembellished architectural style. He is buried in Westminster Abbey, but not in the Poets' Corner.

Rennie made no pretensions to poetising, but famous poets have often done considerably worse than he.

Drummond of Hawthornden was one of the ornaments of a poetic age. But when Ben Jonson came to visit him, this was the level of their inspiration.

"Welcome, welcome, royal Ben."

"Thank ye, thank ye, Hawthornden."

It seems that Drummond was excellent when it pleased him, both in English and Latin, but he balanced this by the extreme badness of his doggerel. On being refused entry to the town of Forfar (the town of sutors or brogue-makers), on the grounds that he was a poet, a profession that was abhorrent to the Presbyterian God, he turned his steed across the Muir Moss, a wretched road, to Kirriemuir. Here he was made warmly welcome, for the simple reason that "Thrums" was at daggers drawn with Forfar. In repayment of their hospitality, Drummond left the weavers this sample of his word-weaving.

"The Kirriemuirians met the Forfarians at the Muir Moss,
The Kirriemuirians beat the Forfarians back to the cross.
Sutors ye are and sutors will be—
Fye upon Forfar.—Kirriemuir bears the gree."

The only excuse for this rubbish is that the first two lines are equal in length, if not in strength, to the longest lines in Latin or Greek poetry.

The passing of time cannot be blamed for cheapening this stuff. It was never good, and never meant to be. Unhappily the same cannot be said for much good poetry, which constant reiteration and advertising in the media has devalued.

Blair, minister of Athelstaneford, was author of a moralising poem, "The Grave." Burns' favourite passage from it begins,

"Friendship, mysterious cement of the soul;"the emphasis, at that time, being on the first syllable of cement. But the passage of two centuries has winded it past remedy and today it is merely ludicrous.

Jonathan Swift when challenged could do a lot better than this. At a literary gathering he was being praised for his rhyming ability when a Scotch lady, an aggressively fiery red-head, defied him to find a rhyme for her name. He asked what it was, expecting a name perhaps like MacGillechionich, but it was nothing more exotic than Mrs Humbie, an East Lothian parish name. Without a pause the witty dean replied,

"You make a mistake
If you think I can't make
A rhyme for your name, Mistress Humbie.
Since the hair on your head
Is so flamingly red
How red must the hair on your bum be."

Robert Fergusson, when a young student at St Andrews, was equally apt. He was called in his turn to say grace. The main course was rabbit, as it had been for months. Before anyone could stop him, he recited,

"For rabbits young, rabbits old,
For rabbits hot, rabbits cold,
For rabbits tender, rabbits tough
Our thanks we render,
We've had enough.   Amen."

When James VI and I visited Linlithgow, the birthplace of his mother, Mary Queen of Scots, a dramatic welcome was arranged for him. The schoolmaster, Mr James Wiseman, was put inside a plaster lion, and met James as he entered the town. He addressed him thus,—

"Thrice, royal sir, here do I you beseech
Who art a lion, to hear a lion's speech.
A miracle: for since the days of Aesop
No lion till those days a voice dared raise up
To such a Majesty. Then, King of men,
The King of Beasts speaks to thee from his den,
Who, though he now enclosed be in plaister,
When he was free was Lithgow's wise schoolmaister."

It is only a step from the sublime to the ridiculous, and many a good poet has slipped and only pulled himself back in time; but, if his slip has been spotted, the public got a good laugh for a long time. This happened to James Thomson, a native of Roxburghshire, author of the "Seasons." When a young man he put on a play in Drury Lane, the title "Sophonisba." On the first night there was a good house. Everything went well until the hero declaimed the line,

"O Sophonisba, Sophonisba O."

at which a broad Scots voice bawled out from the stalls,

"O, Jemmy Thomson, Jemmy Thomson, O."

which brought the house down.

On the second night the line had become

"O Sophonisba, I am wholly thine."

John Home, a Scottish clergyman, wrote the play "Douglas" with the famous lines, "My name is Norval, On the Grampian Hills my father kept his flocks," and was promptly discharged by the General Assembly to whom all art was anathema. But the play aroused such great enthusiasm that a patriotic Scot cried out, "Whaur's your Willie Shakespeare noo?", a remark which also brought the house down.

It is said that an English gentleman asked sarcastically, "Was Shakespeare not a Scotsman then?" to which a stern Caledonian replied gravely, "No, man, and that's a great peety, for unquestionably the man had the abeelity to maintain oor reputation."

Charles Lamb attended a Burns' Supper in Scotland some twenty years after the bard's death. He congratulated the organisers and complimentarily remarked "What a pity it is that Burns himself could not have been present at such a convivial gathering." To which a grave Scot reprovingly answered, "But Mister Lamb, that's impossible, for the man's deid."

Seven cities claimed Homer dead, we are told. It is the same in Scotland. Many places are proud to have been the birthplace of poets, no matter though, when alive, they had to beg their bread there, and indeed, died of starvation in some cases.

Nearly seventy years ago a very expensively produced volume "The Glasgow Poets" was published. Anthologies make strange bedfellows, and there is a queerly mixed company there. One of the earliest of Glasgow's bards was Zachary Boyd, a learned divine who tempted Providence by reducing much of the Bible to verse. But only here and there, as in the story of Jonah, does he slip into ludicrous lines like:

"What house is this where's neither coal nor candle
Where I no thing but guts of fishes handle?"
His enemies made parodies of Boyd and tagged on things he never wrote just
as they do now with McGonagall.
Boyd never wrote,
"There was a man called Job
Dwelt in the land of Uz.
He had a good gift of the gob;
The same case happens us."
or this,
"And Jacob made for his wee Josie
A tartan coat to keep him cosie
And what for no? There was nae harm
To keep the lad baith saft and warm."
The strict Calvinists when practising psalms and paraphrases on weekdays
would not use even Boyd's versions but made up silly rhymes like
"Behold how good a thing it is
And how exceeding great
To run along the garden wall
And swing upon the gate."
The best-known satire (sung to a psalm-tune), too long to print in full, was
"The Cameronian Cat." which was hanged for catching a mouse upon the
Sabbath day.
"There was an auld Seceder's cat
Gaed hunting for a prey.
And ben the hoose she catched a moose
Upon the Sabbath Day."

The best of Glasgow's poets was Thomas Campbell who was a most
remarkable man, small, neat, witty. One of his famous poems, "The Soldier's
Dream," which I learned at school, he thought very poorly of, "Scarcely worth
the cursing," he wrote.
His Hohenlinden (he was present at the battle), ends two verses with the line,
"Of Iser rolling rapidly," After a night out, one of Campbell's friends slipped on
the staircase, and, when asked what the noise was, said:
"Tis I, sir, rolling rapidly."

Dougal Graham, the Glasgow Skellat Bellman or Town Crier, wrote a verse
account of the '45 Rising which he witnessed as a sutler in the Jacobite army. But
on returning to Glasgow, which had suffered from the Highlanders, he turned
his coat, and took to making fun of "her nainsels," the Gaelic speaking followers
of Prince Charlie.
His best comical satires are "John Highlandman's Remarks on Glasgow,"
"Tugal MacTaggart", and "The Turnimspike." He has been copied ever since in
his imitation of the Gael's attempt at Scots.
"Hersel' pe Highland shentleman
Pe auld as Pothwell Prig, sir,
And mony alterations seen
Amang the Lawland whig, sir."
Glasgow has always had a love-hate attitute to its ancient foes, but it is not
taken seriously. Here is an old ditty about the 42nd Highlanders.

"Wha saw the 42nd,
Wha saw them gaun awa'
Wha saw the 42nd
Marchin' to the Broomielaw.
Some o' them had tartan breeches
Some o' them had nane ava
Some o' them had kiltie cauld bums
Marchin' to the Broomielaw."

The wonder is, with its mixture of old enemies, as well as Irish Celts, it is not a less kindly city. But it has a peculiar humour all its own.

Burns suffered, like Zachary Boyd, from posthumous additions to his works, which ring false to any ear attuned to genuine Burns. He certainly had a habit of scratching verses, often not very inspired, on window panes, but a traditional one I heard lately, said to have referred to an inn on Gala Water, I cannot credit. Burns had been overcharged at Torsonce Inn and is said to have complained in these lines.

"If e'er again I gaan this road
This bugger's hoose I'll mind, be Goad;
Three and ninepence for a dinner,
O the damned infernal sinner."

I know, from boyhood, many of these ascribed verses, and I repeated them to an academic American lady seeking the folk-memories of Burns; the research was *not* for additions to Burns' works, but to trace the lingering unprinted tradition.

A famous one is this, said to have been uttered in anger by Burns on finding his hostelry occupied by prostitutes.

"Here's me, Rabbie Burns, just fresh frae the ploo,
I earn my breid in the sweit o' my broo,
But you dirty bitches are just the reverse,
Ye earn your breid in the sweit o' your erse."

There are many of a like nature, none of them any more bawdy than his "Merry Muses of Caledonia," but not admitted to that collection. They are rather like the rude epitaphs which abound all over Scotland, but which never by any chance can be found on a tombstone.

The scene is the kirkyaird. Two local housewives are reading the epitaph.

"Here lies John Broon, an honest merchant in this toon;
Full fourteen pounds his stones did weigh, whether for meal or coal,
Thirty six inches was his yard. God rest his honest soul."

The ladies commented: "Aye, those were the days when we women got justice."

Mr Taylor, dominie of Currie, Midlothian, caused Burns to laugh heartily when he read out a few verses from his book of manuscripts, particularly the passage on the title page, which was also meant for his own epitaph, apparently.

"Rin, bookie, rin, roond the warld lowp,
Whilst I lie in the yaird wi' a cauld dowp."

He recommended Burns to the extent of saying, "The lad'll do. Considering his want o' lear, he's well eneuch."

Burns wrote some pithy epitaphs, for the living more than for the dead, and it seems that some malicious or joking rhymesters attributed their efforts to poor Rabbie. Here are two:

On Dr Gordon, who had an uncommon large mouth.
"Here lies the body of Doctor Gordon
Teeth a' mighty and mooth accordin'.
Stranger tread lichtly on this wonner
If he opens his mooth, ye're gone by thunner."

On a notorious miser:
"Inter'd beneath this kirkyaird stane
Lies stingy Jimmy Wyatt
He died ane morning just at ten
And saved a denner by it."

This may have been about Rob Roy, but, as there were many red-haired Roberts, it could have applied to others:
"In the Last Day when ithers rise
Lie still, Red Rob, gin ye be wise."

The prize for bathos must surely go to this rhyming finale to an epitaph in Tranent,
"Trumpets shall sound, archangels cry,
Come forth Is'bel Mitchell and meet
William Matthison in the sky."

Walter Scott wrote an epitaph for his gamekeeper and general factotum (former poacher), but, though neither in verse, nor on a stone, it is poetic as well as humorous.
"Here lies one who could be trusted with untold gold
But never with unmeasured whisky."

A Border farmer who, like King Lear, had unwisely divided his estate up among his family, is said to have left this epitaph, which we hope, was read by his ungrateful children.
"I, John Bell, leave here a mell (heavy hammer)
The man to fell,
Who leaves a' to his bairns,
And keeps nocht to himsel."

And another of that violent race, the "Bloody Bells," put this upon his stone in Sark Kirkyaird, a few miles from Gretna Green.
"I, Jocky Bell o' Brackenbrow,
Lie under this stane.
Five o' my ain sons laid it on my wame.
I lived a' my deys but sturt and strife,
Was man o' my meat and master o' my wife.
If you've done better in your dey than I did in mine
Tak this stane off my wame and lay it on thine."

The most famous epitaphs never disgraced a tombstone, but are usually the work of anonymous bards. One of these is,
"Here lies the body of Mary MacGurney
Fell off a tramcar and broke her journey."

A very unusual verse was once heard in a Glasgow shop about the time of the failure of the Glasgow bank last century. A gentleman walked into the shop and extended a £1 note, saying as he laid the suspect note on the counter,

"Good-day, Mr Scott
Have ye change o' this note?"
The shopkeeper answered,
"I'm no very sure
But I'll see . . .
I'm afraid, Mr Dewar
It's no' in my pooer
For my wife's gane awa wi the key."

Culloden House, home of President Duncan Forbes, was renowned for hospitality. A friend, Hector Scott, was entertained very lavishly with Ferintosh whisky (which the Forbeses had been granted permission to distil) and fell under the table, as every gentleman was expected to do. Duncan was still on his feet, and able to remember enough of the Homeric tale to address Scott thus,

"Hector, arise, thou mighty son of Priam."
To which Scott replied, despite his state,
"Was ever mortal man as drunk as I am?"

Anonymous geniuses were at work all over Scotland rhyming on natural objects. At least their poems had a practical use, and were brief and to the point. It has been said that the most useful poem in English is that beginning, "Thirty days hath September," which need never have been written had Caesar Augustus, out of sheer jealousy of his uncle Julius, not upset the regular calendar by making August as long as July.

But the rustic rhymes are useful if one wishes to remember, say, the Border rivers.

"The Etterick
And the Slitterick
The Feeder
And the Leader
The Talla
And the Gala
The Ale
And the Kale
The Yod
And the Jed
The Blackadder
The Whitadder
The Teviot and the Tweed."
or the life-saving hint that still waters run deep, proved by the Scots, retreating from Flodden, to their cost.

Said Tweed to Till
"What gars ye rin sae still?"
Said Till to Tweed
"Tho ye rin wi' speed
And I rin slaw
Where ye droon ae man
I droon twa."

91

Practically every mile of some areas in Scotland had a prophetic rhyme, by Thomas the Rhymer, or the Brahan Seer, or some person on whom their cloak fell: some of these came true, and some are still to be fulfilled, and many were only wishful thinking, like this, aimed at James II's crime of treacherously slaying the young Earl of Douglas.

"Edinburgh Castle toor and toun
God grant ye sink for sin
E'en for that Black Dinner
Earl Douglas gat therein."

We descend now to the level of the village green and midden, for even these lowly places had their bards. A simple rhyme often bites deeper and lasts longer than a stone-mason's inscription.

A local Don Juan in Berwickshire, who had been around a bit, left this thumb-nail sketch of the village maidens.

"The lasses o Lauder are mim and meek,
The lasses o the Fanns smell o peat reek,
The lasses o Gordon canna sew a steek
But weel can they sup their crowdie.
The lasses o Earlston are bonnie and braw,
The lasses o Greenlaw are black as a craw,
But the lasses o Polwart are best o them a'
And gie plenty wark to the howdie." (i.e. they often required the midwife)

Dr Henderson, of Chirnside, printed his life-time notes on Berwickshire sayings in Newcastle, in 1855. I think the Scottish printers of that Victorian era would be too priggish to print the honest doctor's work, which was often "plainer than plain" and is a refreshing oasis in a wilderness of hypocrites.

The local verses on "Clarty Kirsten" are too long to publish here, two may suffice as samples.

"She didna wash her sharny nieves
Afore she kirned the butter.
Clarty Kirsten's hame-made cheese
Gied Hielandmen the skitter."

and in the same fatalist spirit as "Ilkley Moor," where a sad fate was foretold to a young man, Clarty Kirsten showed her spite at pretty lasses.

"She didna loe a bonnie lass,
Says she, "It's gey weel kenned
Hooever braw ye are ye'll pass
To coo-shites in the end."

Dr Henderson charitably remarks, "She was a complete earthworm;" but

"She is gane, she is gane,
Where the gerss is ever green,
And there's nae distinction drawn
Betwixt the clarty and the clean."

and on this sober note our rhapsody draws to a close.

But before we end the chapter we must clear McGonagall and Burns of two false attributes.

MacGonagall did not write,

"As I was going along the road
I met a coo—a bull, by Goad."

92

nor did Burns write this libel on our four-legged friend;
  The Cuddie
"The cuddie runs aboot the braes,
      Nane smugger.
And keichs on a' the neebours' claes,
      The bugger."

A whole volume would not be enough to tell about the parish rhymers of Scotland. Glasgow and Hawick, Paisley and Dundee, and many smaller places, were said to have "mair poets than polis." Rhyming was a national hobby starting in childhood. Marjory Fleming, known in Walter Scott's circle as "Pet Marjory", was a quaint little poetess whose story and poems were collected by Dr John Brown. They well merit reading even today, though she died of measles when only eight years old, before Waterloo. The Scots, least of all nations, deserve to be called prosaic.

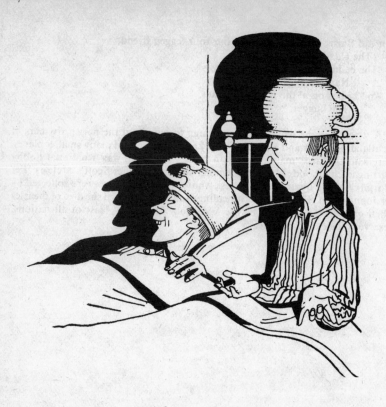

FOOLS AND FOLLIES

The gravest fish is an oyster
The gravest bird is an owl
The gravest beast is an ass
And the gravest man is a fool.

So runs an old rhyme, which Burns probably had in mind when he wrote, "Ye are sae grave, nae doot ye're wise."

Mankind has been exhorted to seek wisdom, but the entire history of man tells that fools have always been a bigger attraction than wise men, one proverbial reason being that "a fool may give a wise man council."

In some countries fools pass unnoticed, for the general level of wisdom is not very high. Barnum said that there was a fool born every minute, and he used this knowledge, as do many con-men, to his own advantage. In Scotland, where intellect was highly respected, one would have thought that simpletons would have had a rough time, but such was not the case; not, at least among the sensible body of citizens. Children had little sense and especially in the slums of the Lowland cities, "the dafties" had a wretched life, plagued by swarms of young brats, who did not spare anyone, whether physically or mentally handicapped. As these brats grew up, most of them learned better manners, and if they didn't, the so-called fools frequently got the better of them.

94

Probably the most famous of all the "dafties" was the unfortunate "Daft Jamie" of Edinburgh, who was one of the victims of the murderers, Burke and Hare, described in a couplet of the times as

The ruffian dogs—the hellish pair—
The villain Burke—the meagre Hare—

When the trial of these scoundrels brought to light the details of their atrocities, all Scotland, and indeed all Britain, was more in a humour to shed tears over the fate of "Daft Jamie" than to laugh at his antics and slyness. Nevertheless several hawkers, pedlars and patterers carried coarsely printed chap-books, containing the biography and sayings of "Daft Jamie", who was more sincerely and universally mourned than any of the Royal Family who died at that time.

Here is a sample of his quaint humour.

He was very fond of asking conundrums and was highly delighted when he got the answer, "I gie it up," and he had to tell them. Here are some of his favourite guesses.

Q. In what month of the year do the ladies talk least?
A. February, for there are least days in it.

Q. Why is a jailer like a musician?
A. Because he maun tak' care o' his key.

Q. What is the cleanest meat a dirty cook can mak ready?
A. A hen's egg, for she canna get his dirty fingers in it.

Q. What is the answer to this?
     Tho' I black and dirty am,
     An black as black can be;
     There's many a lady that will come,
     An by the haun tak me.

This was such a well-known guess that a bystander sometimes said, tantalisingly "I ken your guess, Jamie, it's a tea-kettle." At this Jamie would be so vexed that he would run away crying, "Because ye ken, because somebody telt ye."

Someone asked Jamie "Why do ladies not generally carry Bibles to Kirk?"

"Because they're ashamed o' themsels for they canna fin' oot the text," he replied, with a good deal of truth.

Jamie had a half-wit friend, Robert Kirkwood, known as Bobby Awl. One cold day they felt they would be the better of a drink of whisky. Bobby had twopence, Jamie fourpence. When the drink was on the counter. Bobby pretended to Jamie that there was a dog-fight outside in the street. When Jamie went out to see it, Bobby drank both glasses.

Jamie on re-entering said "What's come o' the whisky, ye daft beast? Ye've drunk it a' and left me nane."

Bobby replied, "Och I was dry and couldna wait."

When Jamie was asked why he did not revenge himself for this trick he answered "What could I say to puir Bobby? He's daft, ye ken."

Poor innocent souls. Their lives were equally cut short when the world could ill spare them. Bobby was killed by the kick of a donkey, and Jamie suffocated by the thugs when he was 19. Both their bodies ended up on the doctors' dissecting table.

There was a difference between a fool and a jester, the latter being an official provided with clothing and having a certain dignity. As time went on the two offices ran into one. Several Scottish lairds and nobles had their jesters until comparatively modern times. The Earl of Strathmore had a jester who died in 1787. His coat and hat are still to be seen at Glamis Castle. The Laird of Udny was not a great nobleman, but he kept a fool named James Fleming, or Jeemie Fleeman, whose wise sayings exceed his foolish ones. He was "no fool for himself." He pretended not to know the value of money, but to judge all coins by their size. When a native of the district (whom he was likely to meet again) offered him the choice between a penny and a sixpenny piece, he always said "I'll tak' the big yin." This highly amused everyone so he was often approached to make this choice.

But if a stranger came to him, to give him the same choice, he used to pretend to be very virtuous, and would say coyly, "I'll no be greedy. I'll tak the wee yin."

He was seen puzzling himself over a horse-shoe, turning it over and over, and shaking his head sadly. A local wiseacre came along.

"What's this queer-like thing?" asked the natural.

"You must be a richt daftie no tae ken that it's a horse-shoe."

"Lord sakes," observed Jeemie," what it is to be a wyce man, and to ken at a gliff that it's no a mare's shoe."

Jeemie Fleeman got the credit for other men's follies as well as his own, but several are his own property.

He managed to get a meaty leg of roast mutton from a farmer's wife and walked along taking a bite now and again. He sat by a bridge to finish his gnawing. The laird came along and remarked in passing, "Aye, Jeemie, it's a grand-like day, is't no?"

Jeemie was not always spoken to by important folk, so he looked up sourly and said, "O, aye, ye ken a body when he has onything."

The laird was surveying a large field, which had just been harrowed, and was discussing with the farmer and the factor whether he would put it down to grass, barley or oats.

"I wonder what would thrive best here? The soil's a bit unkindly and stony."

Jeemie broke in, "Saw it wi factors, laird. They're bound to thrive onywhere."

A prosperous miller in Udny, who was suspected of taking an over-large multure from his customers, asked Jeemie contemptuously, "Fleeman, d'ye ken onything ava?"

Fleeman replied, "Some things I ken and some I dinna ken."

"What dae ye ken?" asked the miller.

"I ken that a miller has aye a big fat soo."

"And what do ye no ken?"

"I dinna ken whase expense she's fed at."

Fleeman's best joke was also very brief. An inquisitive man asked him, "Are you Jeemie Fleeman, Udny's fool?" "Aye," he replied "Fa's feel are ye?"

A pompous professor of Aberdeen met a fool, and asked him the rather personal question, "How long will a man live without brains?" But in the typical Scots way the "natural" replied with another question, "Hoo auld are ye yersel, professor?"

In the Forfarshire kirk on a warm summer morning a good many of the congregation succumbed to the droning of the sermon and fell asleep. The minister thought he would give them a notable reproof, so he stopped his sermon and pointed to Daft Jamie Fraser, who was wide awake.

"Ye see even the puir eediot Jamie Fraser is wide awake, while the rest o' ye are asleep."

Jamie replied in a loud voice, "And gin I hadna been an eediot I wad hae faen asleep tae."

Our ancestors suffered fools gladly, and the fools appear to have had a good time, for they were quite able to look after their own interests and provide amusement into the bargain.

An Edinburgh minister, like many others, included fools and idiots in his concluding prayer. He was in duty bound also to pray for the powers-that-be, so he did not forget them either.

"Lord , hae mercy on all fools and eediots, and particularly on the Toon Cooncil o' Edinburgh."

The fools were best remembered when they turned the tables on their supposed superiors.

A Border "Daft Jamie" had long legs and tough feet, and he used to take passengers pick-a-back over the Teviot below Hawick. One day the Laird of Cavers and his brother asked to be carried over. The Laird's brother liked a joke, so he gave Jamie a shilling to drop his brother in mid-stream. Sure enough in the deepest part Jamie said, "My cuit's kittley. I maun scratch it." The Laird said, "Can ye no wait till we get ower?" But Jamie couldn't wait to scratch his heel. He plumped the Laird in the current and went back for the brother, who was laughing heartily. However, when they came again to mid-stream, Jamie said, "Gie me twa shilin's or in ye go. What was guid for the Laird canna do ye ony herm." And the practical joker had to fork out.

Many tales of "Feels", as the Buchan tongue has it, were transferred from one place to another.

One of these 'feels' was invited into the kitchen of the big hoose for dinner. He had a voracious appetite, so he set about a bowl of broth in style. He then began on a pot of 'rumble-de-thumps' or potatoes mashed up with vegetables and butter. After that, a suet pudden, in the midst of which he was heard to say, looking up to heaven, "O, Lord A'michty, swadge me, swadge me, or I rive." (Satisfy me before I burst.)

Another house was not so generous and he soon polished off his helping, which was served on an ordinary plate. He was asked if he was satisfied. He shook his head.

"What would you like then?"

He pointed to a large ashet, or serving dish.

"Mair o' the same on a mair plate."

A bull on the rampage came running up the road and everyone leapt the nearest fence, but the fool got down on his hands and knees and pretended to chew the grass, crying out, "Moo! Moo!" After the bull had gone out of sight, the other folk came back and asked why he had indulged in such antics.

"I was lettin' on I was a coo, till I could get oot o' the bull's gait."

97

Another daft fellow, who confused things a bit, supplies this tale.

A painter and glazier was employed in a large institution to mend windows. He collected the old putty and broken glass in a sack and went down to the shrubbery to dump it. In the shrubbery he found an inmate trying to break his way through the wall with a fore-hammer, making quite a din.

"What are you doing?" asked the glazier.

"Ssh," cautioned the hammer-man, "They'll hear ye. I'm trying to brak lowse. Can ye help me?"

He began to swing the hammer threateningly so the glazier said he had a plan to help him. He emptied out the putty and glass and invited the man to get into the sack, saying, "I'll walk out past the porter's lodge and let you out of the sack when we get away. You understand?"

At the gate the porter asked what was in the sack. "Broken glass."

Just to make sure the porter gave the bottommost bulge of the sack a hefty kick, whereupon the contents of the sack cried out in a loud voice, "Tinkle! Tinkle!"

Domestic contrivances often puzzled simpletons. Some time about the turn of the century two country lads went for a holiday in London. They got up to their hotel room and made ready for bed. The maid, remembering that she had not furnished them with chamber-pots, knocked at the door, handed in the pots, and waggishly remarked, "Your night-caps, gentlemen."

They had never seen such sumptuous articles before, but decided they would follow the custom of the capital. They put them on their heads and lay down to sleep. But for some reason sleep eluded them. After half-an-hour one of them lit a candle and sat up in bed.

"I canna sleep wi' this thing on my heid," he drooled.

His friend, peering at him from beneath his porcelain helmet, laughed.

"Nae wunner, ye silly ass, ye've got the bow at the back."

A Wigton half-wit, who always carried a long staff, saw a funeral party, the mourners on horseback. He bestrode his staff like a hobby-horse and tried to keep up with them for a mile or two, through very muddy roads. At the graveyard Daft Jock came up with the hearse and mourners.

"Guid sakes, sirs," he panted, "if it hadna been for the fashion o' the thing to ride to the burial, I wad hae been as weel to hae come on my ain feet."

It is not often that the minister is made out to be a fool. In a rural parish the minister called at a small farm, but found the only one at home was the grandmother, Mrs Thomson. He asked how all the family were keeping, and if he might offer up a prayer for any that were ailing. The old lady said that the only one that ailed anything was Davie.

On the Sabbath a titter went round the congregation when he prayed for Davie Thomson's speedy recovery. He could not understand this irreverence until the next time he called at the Thomsons, to ask how Davie was. "Ach, dinna be daft, meenister. Davie's the cuddy."

Mirrors of glass were uncommon in outlying places. There was a superstition against breaking one, but this arose more from the scarcity than any other reason.

Glenesk was an isolated part of Angus, far into the Grampians, and the people

98

rarely ventured down to the coast, but one man did travel as far afield as Stonehaven, where he went into a hotel to have his dinner.

On the opposite side of the dining-room was a mirror, a contrivance he had never seen before. He looked up and saw a figure with a beard and bonnet similar to his own, also having his dinner.

He called out to it, "Ye may ken ye're a Glenesk man, by your scraggy face."

A piece of mirror was cast up among some wreckage on the shore of a little Hebridean island, whose only inhabitants were a simple couple who had never been on the mainland. The man picked up the mirror and looked at it.

"Eh, is that no' a strange thing? A photy o' my faither. It's his speaking likeness. What a handsome man he must have been."

He took the photo back and hid it in a drawer, going back every now and again to admire it. His wife grew suspicious, and when she saw him safely off to the peats, she stole away to the drawer and took out the mirror. Her suspicions were fully justified.

"The blagyaird." she exclaimed. "A photy o' anither wumman. And an uglier lookin' bitch I've ne'er clappit my een on."

Sorn is an upland parish of Ayrshire but its inhabitants are very quick-witted. A young lad from Sorn was apprenticed to an undertaker in Ayr. His employer, anxious to put the simple country lad at ease in the strange bustle of the county town, began to ask him about his native parish.

"Where div ye come frae, my lad?"

"I bide up at Sorn."

"A healthy upland district, eh?"

"O, aye, gey healthy roon oor parish."

"Folk'll no dee vera often there, eh?"

"Na, just aince."

Isaac Disraeli says that Tom-o'-Bedlam men, wandering madmen, disappeared after the Civil War, and remarks wryly that he did not know so many Roundheads and Cavaliers were recruited from this source. But in all ages many a witless soul has been enlisted in the army.

A simple Scots recruit was being questioned by the medical officer.

"How are your bowels, my man?" he barked.

To the Scot this meant kitchenware.

"We've no been issued wi' them yet, sir."

"No, no, I mean, are you constipated?"

"Certainly not, sir. I'm a volunteer."

"Good God, man. Don't you know the king's English?"

"Is he?"

The laird of a certain Border parish was a "queerish" fellow, an eccentric, but no-one dared tell him so to his face, for he had a stout ash-plant he was fairly free with.

One autumn day he spied one of his humbler tenants perched up on a roof, thatching it with wheat straw.

"See ye mak a guid job o' that theikin, John," he cried.

"I'll dae that sir."

Then a bit jocularly the laird took off his cap, exposing a bald pate.

"D'ye think ye could theik that, John?"

"Na, laird," cried John from his safe station, "That's beyond me. It's a slate ye need."

A chapter on fools and follies would be incomplete without an account of some of the humours of the reign of James VI and I. The king himself has been nicknamed "The Wisest Fool in Christendom" but this is a title which has very little meaning, except to say that his character was a strange mixture of wisdom and folly. As he managed to avoid going to war all through his reign in England of over twenty years, he must have been no fool; yet he was fond of fooling and had many fools at court.

In a book "The Court of James," a contemporary, Weldon, has given us a scandalous picture of the behaviour of the Stewart King after he quit Scotland and came into his fortune. Here is one description:

"After the King supped, he would come forth to see pastimes and fooleries; in which Sir Ed. Zouch, Sir George Goring and Sir John Finit were the chief and master fools, and surely this fooling got them more than any other's wisdom. Zouch's part was to sing bawdy songs and tell bawdy tales. Finit's to compose those songs: there was a set of fiddlers brought to court on purpose for this fooling, and Goring was the master of games for these fooleries, sometimes presenting David Droman and Archee Armstrong, the King's fool, on the back of other fools to tilt at one another until they fell together by the eares: sometimes they performed antic dances. But Sir John Millicent (who was never known before) was commended for notable fooling and was indeed the best contemporary fool of them all."

But James was not always in a mood to appreciate fooling. Once when he was melancholy over affairs of state the Duke of Buckingham, "his humble slave and dogge," thought to cheer him up.

He got a young lady to bring in a piglet dressed in infant's clothing. Buckingham's mother carried it to the King, dressed in a rich mantle. A man Turpin, robed as a bishop in all his ornaments, began the rites of baptism with the Book of Common Prayer in one hand and a silver ewer with water in the other. Buckingham stood as godfather. When James turned to look at the child, the piglet squealed. Now, pigs were animals that James had a horror of, as they were associated with the devil, and unclean. He was highly displeased and shouted, "Out! Away! for shame! What blasphemy is this?" Yet James had been delighted at more blasphemous fooleries than this.

It is amusing to compare Jamie the Sax of Scotland with James I of England. In Scotland before he arrived "at the Land of Promise" he had been more repressive. One of his edicts was that "louping, jumping, fitba, gowff and sic other ungodlike games shall be utterlie cried down and not usit." But when he came to Merrie England he had to sing a different tune; "No lawful recreation shall be barred to our good people." The English, like the Scots, liked a "roaring good time," and felt they deserved it. Fooling of all sorts was in their tradition.

Archie Armstrong was the fool of James VI and I, and also of Charles I. How he came to this privileged position is interesting.

Up in the hills, between Jedburgh and Liddesdale, a man was observed to kill a sheep and carry it away on his shoulders. The owners of the flock gathered a band together and set off in pursuit of the thief. A few miles farther on, there was no sign of him, but they saw a small cottage in a wood. They approached it, knocked and entered. A figure in a woman's gown and hood sat by the fireside rocking an infant in a cradle. They were about to leave this innocent scene of domestic bliss when one of them peered into the cradle. The "babe" had a sheep's head and the cradle-rocker was the thief. He was taken to Jedburgh, where rough justice was the rule, and he would no doubt have been hanged, but as it happened King James was in the town on one of his circuits. He heard of the humorous incident so he sent for the thief, Archie Armstrong. The king told him he would grant him respite to repent of his sins, and asked him how he would employ his last days on earth. Armstrong said he would read the Bible, end to end. James promised that his life would be spared until this sacred task was done. Archie replied, "Then deil a single word o't will I set eyes on," at which the King was amused and took him as his fool.

Armstrong wrote a book entitled "Archie's Jests," which Isaac Disraeli describes as "very high priced and of little worth."

James himself seems to have been an unpredictable man. This enabled him to be a step ahead of his innumerable enemies at home and abroad. He acted the fool and encouraged others to do so, but was sometimes extremely shrewd and unprincipled.

The Spanish Ambassador in London had a mania. He thought that language was unnecessary, and that signs would serve as well as words. James decided to take a rise out of the grave senor. He told him that in the most northerly of the British Universities, that of Aberdeen, there was a Professor of Signs. But this eminent man lived six hundred miles away, which made it almost impossible to visit him.

The Spaniard replied, "Were it ten thousand leagues I would set out immediately to confer with this wonderful man."

James, unable to prevent the ambassador setting out, sent a messenger to tell the Aberdeen professoriate to find a professor of signs. They were at their wits' end as to how this was to be done, and had not solved the problem when the ambassador arrived, so they put off the evil day by saying the Professor of Signs was absent in the country, indefinitely. However the indefatigable don said he would wait for his return.

Alarmed at the expense of maintaining their guest and his entourage they approached a local butcher, Geordie, who was blind in one eye, and a witty rogue, and told him the crisis they were in. For a small sum he agreed to be Professor of Signs.

He was made up like a professor, placed in a chair of state, and warned not to speak whatever happened.

In goes the ambassador. He holds up one finger, Geordie holds up two. The Spaniard holds up three; Geordie holds up a clenched fist and looks fierce. The embassador holds up an orange he had in his pouch. Geordie holds up a barley-scone. The interview is over.

"What did you think of him?" asked the professors anxiously, of the ambassador.

"A perfect miracle. I held up a finger to denote there is one God; he held up two to signify the Father and Son. I held up three meaning the Trinity; he clenched his first to mean these three were one. I took out an orange to mean God gives us necessities and luxuries; he held up a piece of bread, the staff of life, preferable to all luxuries." The ambassador departed highly delighted.

Geordie was now asked to give his account.

"The scoundrel. He held up ae finger, meaning I'd but ae ee. I held up twae fingers as muckle as say my ee was as guid as his twae. Then he held up three fingers to mean there was but three amang us. I stickit my neive to gie him a whack but I held back for your sakes. Then he took oot an orange, to mean auld beggarly Scotland canna grow thae, but I showed him a whang o' barley bannock to show how little I cared for his foreign trash."

This tale shows that a learned man can be as big a fool as an ignoramus. "There was never a goose withoot a gander."

The Wise Men of Gotham near Nottingham had their Scottish counterparts in the Gowks o' Gordon, Berwickshire, and the Scholars of Buckhaven, Fife.

The Men of Gotham committed follies to evade their taxes, but the Gowks of Gordon appear to have been genuinely simple-minded, as were the Buckhaveners; or to be just, their neighbours maliciously invented these absurdities.

This fishing village was at one time said to be so peculiar in every way that it was unique among all the fishing communities in Fife. It was a chaos of houses, gardens, middens, boats, nets and old anchors; the inhabitants were rude in speech and manners, and clownish in every respect. But they were so expert at fishing that they were all wealthy. Their peculiarities were satirised early in the 18th century in a pamphlet entitled, "The History of Buckhaven comprising the sayings of Wise Willie and Witty Eppie and an account of their college (University)." As a result of this publicity Buckhaven was looked on as "The Gotham of Scotland" fit to rival the "Gowks of Gordon". The "University" was an old-fashioned house of two storeys, with outside stairs facing the shore. The probable reason for this ill-treatment of Buckhaven is that it was founded by Flemish (Brabantine) sailors, survivors of a vessel wrecked here in the 16th century, who spoke and acted in a manner incomprehensible to the natives of Fife. In 1827 Robert Chambers says they seemed to be an industrious, simple, and primitive folk, like all the Fife fishers.

One of the glories of the burgh magistrates that has now departed for ever is the Provost's chain of office. True, it once occasioned a very caustic aside at the annual Burns Supper, when a Provost named Edward got up to speak, his robe bespattered with haggis. A councillor whispered,

"See approach proud Edward's power,
Chains and slaverie."

In a small Aberdeenshire town a visitor was informed that small though it was, the town was a Royal Burgh and had a Provost.

"And does the Provost go about with a chain?" asked the tourist.

"Na, he just gangs aboot loose."

A magistrate of Edinburgh is credited with having committed a kind of treason on a few occasions. When Edward, then Prince of Wales, was living at Holyroodhouse, the provost thought it only hospitable and human to inquire after the health of Queen Victoria, but he could have put it better.

"How's your mother?" he asked.

The rebuke came like a flash of lightning from the "Peacemaker."

"*My* mother, sir! *your* Queen!"

No whit reformed, when Edward was in Perth, one of his official entourage, perhaps the same dropper of clangers, remarked, "Did your highness know that Perth is the most sinful city in all the British Empire?"

Edward had quite a background of seraglios to judge from, so he pretended interested surprise, for Perth seemed a dull respectable city.

"How so?"

"Well, your highness, in almost every street there is a signpost saying 'This way to the Fair Maid's House."

Edward laughed, but not heartily.

Some worthy office-bearers have left a tradition of folly, usually unintentional. The press never reported these: it was left to oral tradition to hand them on.

An Edinburgh Lord Provost was known for his gaffes. He was a homely Scot who spoke the Doric, and was out of his depth with English, and completely submerged with French or Latin.

His high office demanded his presence at a garden party given annually by the City to the "Merchant Maidens." Many notables were present. After tea the company adjourned to play croquet on the lawn. A young lady, flustered by the presence of the baillies and Provost, struck a ball wildly and produced the unladylike spoonerism, "O dear, I've pissed the most;" at which the Provost to cover her retreat, tried out his French, "Ma lassie, I doot ye've made a fu po."

Excusing the delay in putting the new Talla reservoir into use, he addressed the huge protest meeting of ratepayers, as follows: "Ye see we've been maist unfortunate. The engineers took badly, and couldna feenish the conetrack. In fac' the heid yin dee'd." He should have stopped there but he attempted to give particulars and got flustered, "It was gey sudden. He dee'd o' daith." (uproar.)

A Parliamentary Bill was required, to give the City the power to take water from a certain area. At a public meeting some hecklers had expressed doubt about the Bill getting through. The Provost rose to assure the meeting on this point. Had his audience been speakers of Broad Scots they would not have cried out, "O, Provost," in protest at what seemed like vulgarity in English.

"Tak my word for it, this Bill will gang through Parlyment as easy as a pat o' butter slides ower a dug's hass." (Hass is Scots for throat.)

The son of this notable citizen was made a councillor, which excited a good deal of comment, because he had barely come of age, and it was strongly suspected, on good grounds, that undue pressure had been exercised to get the youth into this civic post. There were two rival evening papers in Edinburgh at that time, the Dispatch and the News, the first representing the Tory interest and the second the Radical. Journalists appear to have been more daring in that age, for the first edition of the "News" carried a cartoon showing a naked infant boy, with the features of the Provost's son, under the large caption "Our youngest Councillor." All hell was loose, and the proprietors of the News were more or less forced to retrieve the position by offering a pound for every copy of the first edition returned.

My grandfather kept his copy, which I saw. He valued the exposure of a couple of civic fools above gold.

Baillie Robertson of Musselburgh was a "majestic innocent", who spoke as he thought, without any mealy-mouthed circumlocution.

The Council of the "Honest Toon" had met to discuss burgh affairs of pressing importance.

The provost rose, "Gentlemen, I hae a proposal afore me to build a brig ower the mill-lade."

The Baillie rose, "Ma God, build a brig ower the mill-lade. That's rideeculous. I could piss as far."

"Sit down, baillie," cried the chairman, "You're out of order."

Robertson remained on his feet. "Oot o' order. Oot o' order. I ken fine I'm oot o' order. Gin I was in order I could piss twice as far."

103

If tradition does not lie, this plain language was refined, compared with the abuse that the local fishwives threw about in dispute. But the more refined folk turned a deaf ear to this.

At another council meeting the baillie was in trouble again.

"We hae a petition here frae Mr Hipp, the grocer, asking for permission to open a new branch on the other side o' the High Street, for the convenience o' the Fisherraw folk."

The Baillie rises: "I oppose this on the grounds o' public decency."

The Provost: "I didna think that a small thing like that wad hae worried ye. But hoo does the petition offend decency."

The Baillie: "Weel, gin ye agree to his request ye'll hae his name in big letters baith on the nor' and the sooth sides. I'm no haein' ony man makin' an erse oot o' oor High Street."

Baillie Robertson owned a gig drawn by a chestnut mare, a very smart turn-out. He kept the gig spick and span, and the mare well-fed. One afternoon he was driving up country when he overtook the schoolmistress, so he offered her a lift, which she gladly accepted. They chatted about the weather, the scholars, this and that. Then an incident occurred which horsemen and horsewomen disregard. To put this in ballad form:

> They hadna gane a hunner yairds
> A hunner yairds but three
> When the mare's tail lift, and then she rift,
> Wi a guff like pudden-bree.

To the unrefined baillie this was amusing, but the college-bred lady found his chuckles out of place. In the next two miles this pleasantry was repeated several times. They then reached the road-end where the school-marm was due to descend.

She could not keep silent. "Baillie Robertson, I have never been so insulted in all my life."

The baillie scratched his head in some surprise then it dawned on him.

"Eh, lassie, I ne'er thocht on it in that licht afore. Come on, we'll baith get doon and kick the bitch's erse."

The water-baillie was going his rounds when he spied a fisherman angling on one of the most valuable stretches of the Tweed. He asked him to pull in his line and make himself scarce. The fellow obliged and to the amazement of the baillie revealed a potato on a hook.

"That's all right," beamed the keeper, "Don't disturb yourself. Stay as long as you like and have good sport." The fisher thanked him and flung his bait back into the pool.

That evening the baillie went into the local pub for his "evening." His curiosity was roused by a circle of men gathered round a table, on which lay half-a-dozen fine trout. His friend of the morning was obviously the successful angler.

"Dinna tell me ye caught a' these wi' a tattie."

"Na," replied the daft one. "But I catched you."

Not far from a certain village there were many relics of former ages in the shape of standing-stones, burial mounds and Picts' houses. There was also a recumbent stone of large size, which was more valuable than all the others, being a steady source of drink-money for the men of the village.

104

Quite often a stranger, keen on archaeology, came upon this stone and had his curiosity aroused by the inscription, "Turn me up and I'll tell you more." Unable to lift it, he came to enlist half-a-dozen men with crow-bars to help him, for a consideration. Imagine the frustration of the curious fortune-hunter when the reverse of the stone read, "Lay me down as I was before." As he rewarded his labourers he certainly paid for his folly.

Social dinners are all right if the mixture is good, otherwise you get the sort of thing which happened in the old days in Leith when the noble horse was the source of tractor power, and the not-so-noble carters formed a very large society.

A firm of contractors decided to do the democratic thing, and invite all its carters to a banquet with the office staff and bosses. The carters were asked to come in dinner-jackets, boiled shirts and black bow ties; to their way of thinking, a fancy dress affair. The carters were used to addressing their horses in terms more or less affectionate, but rather too brief, so Auld Willie, reputed a long-winded wag, was chosen to answer the boss's toast which, after a long harangue, ended: "And so, gentlemen, I ask you to be upstanding and drink to the continued prosperity of the firm, in nectah fit for the gods."

The company took off their glasses of the best malt whisky. Auld Willie was nudged to his feet. He self-consciously adjusted his bow-tie. He had never before heard of nectar, and divinity was only useful as an oath. However, he took his cue from the boss; and plunged boldly forward.

"Friends and felly-cairters, I hae muckle pleesure in replying to the toast, for here I am the nicht, dressed up in a neck-tie fit for Jesus Christ."

It is said that "auld wives and bairns mak fools o' physicians," but sometimes the doctors, with their strange names for diseases, make fools out of old wives. Here is a Glasgow "stair-heid" conversation.

Mrs Macwhachle: "What ails your leddy-lodger, I haena seen her for a week."

Mrs MacShuggle: "O, her. She's in bed wi' sciatica."

Mrs Macwhachle: "Michty on us. Thae damned Talianis again."

Another wifie was explaining what sciatica was.

"It's gey painfu', as ye ken, but it's no fatal. It's just a lang-nebbit word for toothache in the sma' o' the back."

Follies were all the rage in the Gothic revival of the late 18th century. Nearly ever nobleman's estate was adorned by a castle, "rotten before it was half-ripe," or a classical building, left half-completed. Oban has a conspicuous monument known as MacCaig's Folly. Edinburgh has Scotland's Disgrace, a folly; the butt-end of a Parthenon. There are minor follies in Edinburgh quite as ludicrous; for example, Brown's Folly, the statue of Edward the Seventh, in an amphitheatre, facing Holyroodhouse: he is dressed in Tudor style with long stockings and short inexpressibles. There is a mounted leaden statue of Charles II, in Roman kilt, crowned with a laurel wreath. He does not look in the least merry.

Less conspicuous in another Scottish burgh there is a bas-relief of Samson slaying the lion. Samson wears 17th century dress, including a ruff with roses on his shoes. His sugar-loaf hat is too tall to be worn within the framework so it hangs over the diminutive lion like a candle-snuffer. Folly is funny enough when it lives only for nine days, but, in stone, it is a perpetual source of amusement.

One of the most remarkable follies in Scotland is only a few yards from the main road to Portobello. It is a "classical tomb of considerable height and beauty" according to James Grant of 'Old and New Edinburgh.' When I was a boy it stood isolated in grassy meadows, but now it is surrounded by bungalows. Not only is the monument strange; an even more bizarre story lies behind it.

William Miller, a wealthy seedsman of Edinburgh, sold all sorts of horticultural aids. When Prince Charlie's army was in the city in 1745, Miller sold them 500 shovels for trenching. (This, by the way, did not cause Charles to be known as the Young Shovelier.) Miller bought Craigentinny Castle and estate. When he was 90, he married an Englishwoman of 50. After a honeymoon in romantic Paris Mrs Miller gave birth to a child, which grew up to inherit the estate and a fortune, but also a thin figure, weak voice, no beard, and all the peculiar habits of a hermaphrodite. Gossip said he was a changeling, which has several meanings including that of a half-wit. Witless or not, he became an M.P. On his death no stranger was allowed to see his naked body. He was buried forty feet deep, and the tomb, known as the Craigentinny Marbles, was placed over him, to await the trump of Gabriel, when all secrets will be revealed.

THE PRACTICAL SCOT

One of the great books of the world, Robinson Crusoe, by Daniel Defoe, was based on the experiences of a Fifer, Alexander Selkirk, or Selcraig, a native of Largo. Although Defoe's genius built the marvellous tale, it was the practical Scot, Selkirk, and his resourcefulness on the desert island, that supplied the foundation of the story. But Selkirk was merely typical of his nation, and any one of ten thousand Scots, marooned far from civilisation, would have reacted as effectively as he did. The Lowland Scots, with many exceptions of course, were for long notable as practical folk. They are helped in this respect by being a "reading people". Illiteracy was despised.

Practical folk are liable to pay great attention to every detail, and indeed, if they were careless about small things, they would not get very far, for genius has been defined as an infinite capacity for taking pains. The danger, as the Scots have found out to their cost, is that ignorant and malicious people are unable to distinguish between carefulness and miserliness. The Scots have got a totally undeserved character of niggardliness or meanness. So much is this taken for granted, that there appears to be only one joke about Scots, and that is about their grasping nature. It is true that Scots, like Jews, are magnanimous enough to laugh at their own expense, but every Scot worthy of the name should repudiate this insult to their national character. My grandfather could never hear a good word spoken about Harry Lauder who, he often repeated, was the "Grand Vulgariser of Scotland". He was referring to his making capital out of the "Aberdeen Joke", or the "Meanness" story.

However, I do not wish to chew the rag too long, so I shall turn now to the humorous side of the practical Scot.

With a view to commemorating Alexander Selkirk, to whom the world owes so much, I think it only fair to his native Fife to start with a hitherto unpublished testimonial to the canny folk of the "Kingdom of Fife", attributed to the humorous pen of Dr David Rorie, author of many such verses.

The Fifer

They say that a Welshman's as clever as hell
And ye whiles hear the word Aiberdeen,
But I'll bet you my life that a fella frae Fife
Would mak baith the tithers look green.

In the coorse o' my travels I've met twa-three folk
What would do ye afore ye said "knife",
But never a man wi' a readier plan
Than a chiel frae the Kingdom of Fife.

Frae that wonderfu' place there's a langheided race
That's kent a' the wide warld ower,
They're aye in the thick o't and neat wi the trick o't
At warsling to place and to power.

To sup wi a Fifer ye need a lang spune,
He's an ee open aye when he sleeps,
And ye ken the Fife kye can knit stockin's forbye
Wi' their horns when eatin' their neeps.

So ca' them a' whistlers and aye if they're daft
It's on the richt side o' their heid,
An' for a fact, in a business transact
Ye're never quite safe till they're deid.

The reason for the pre-eminence of Fife (or Fibh in Celtic) is because this was the most southerly of the Kingdoms of ancient Pictland, and Robert Chambers says all seven kingdoms of the Picts were known as the 'practical Picts.' Apart from a few communities of fishers from Flanders and Friesland, the Fife folk are still basically Pictish. Fife was a royal region; Falkland Palace was the residence of king and court: those that misbehaved were banished to Freuchie, two whole miles away, to a pretty sordid existence, the sentence of expulsion being, "Awa' to Freuchie and fry mice." Fifers of old were expected to live up to a pretty high standard in every way.

Fife would require a whole volume to itself, such is the ingenious nature of the folk of that region. Even the birds and the beasts seem to have been infected by the canny qualities of the human inhabitants. There is a very old saying about the "flyness" of Fife. "Fife! O, aye, that's where the craws fly backwards to keep the stoor oot o' their een."

My examples of practicality come from every part of Scotland, though the Highlands do not provide many tales: the Celtic fringe, though shrewd enough in its own way, does not come much into the picture in this respect.

Halfway between Fife and Edinburgh is the island of Inchkeith which until recently was part of the parish of Kinghorn, so it is an outlying part of Fife. Quite appropriately, then, there are two practical stories connected with it.

The first is the well-known tale of an experiment by the eccentric James VI, to solve the problem, "What was the first language on earth, Greek or Hebrew or Gaelic?" Did Adam greet Eve with "Ciamar a tha sibh"? So as a practical philologist he put a deaf and dumb nurse on Inchkeith with two new-born infants. The results are not recorded. They possibly grew up squalling for their "sea-maws", for the crying of sea-gulls is continuous in Inchkeith.

The French troops that accompanied Mary of Guise, mother of Mary Queen of Scots, called Inchkeith "The Isle of Horses" since horses grew so fat on the rich vegetation there. On which a Scots law lord, accustomed to trying horse thieves, drily remarked, "Aye, and they wad be a bit safer there.'"

Here are true tales about two of Scotland's famous Roberts, Robert the Bruce and Rob Roy, to show that it was never safe to take their funny remarks too lightly, for they were both men of deeds.

Robert the Bruce was very annoyed at the behaviour of Lord Soulis, whom he suspected, rightly, of intriguing with the English. Unlike the English King Henry II, who cried, "Who will rid me of this turbulent priest (i.e. Becket, Archbishop of Canterbury)?" Bruce took the humorous line when his followers asked him what practical measures they could take to stop Lord Soulis. "Ye can boil him if ye like, for a' I care," said Bruce jocularly. But his followers took this literally and did just that, boiling Soulis, wrapped in lead-foil, in a large cauldron. When anyone uttered a threat of violence, even in a jest, Scottish hearers uttered the proverb, "Ye'll be making another Earl Soulis' mistake."

Rob Roy was in some ways romantic, but also eminently practical. A dragoon pursued him and aimed a sword blow which should have cloven Rob to the teeth, for he appeared to wear only a woollen "tammy," but the sword struck iron, for Rob had put a "guid Cu'ross griddle" of cast iron inside it.

The soldier remarked, "Your mither never wrocht ye that bunnet," and continued the chase. Rob cried to his lieutenant in Gaelic, "Has she not a drop in her, Dugal?" referring not to a dram-bottle but a long musket. At which Dugal shot the trooper through the heart.

"Necessity knows no law" is an old saying. In troubled times gunpowder was a necessity and saltpetre was essential to its making. This was collected by scraping it off the walls of caves, tombs and cellars, but it was found that urine when evaporated left saltpetre as a residue, so each morning a strang-ward went round the houses collecting the night-soil. Some citizens of Auld Reekie, crying "Gardy-loo" either before, during, or after throwing it from the window, had no deposits for the strang-ward when he came round in the morning.

Before the days of practical plumbers, life was primitive, especially in the winter-time when the 'little wooden hut' was at the far end of the garden.

In Orkney a party was being held which entailed much merriment, music, and the old sports of eating, drinking, wenching and purging. Mine Host took the ladies aside, ben the hoose, and told them of the Comfort Station arrangements.

"I've pitten twa or three chanties under the bed, ladies, and in ilk ane I've pitten an auld wig in the bottom to deiden the dirl."

For dire necessity of another kind there was an ancient "country seat" in the kailyaird. One lass with stiletto-heels went out to use it. A young man in a hurry, unaware of this, rushed out in the dark, opened the door and was rammed in the guts by the sharp heels, whereupon he yelled out in agony, bringing everyone to his aid. His first intelligible remark was, "What a stupid place to keep a bloody barry."

Scotland has for some unaccountable reason been very unwilling to recognise her practical geniuses. Instead, they are often persecuted and ill-treated. Kirkpatrick MacMillan, inventor and maker of the world's first bicycle in 1839, rode on it into Glasgow, where he was prosecuted and fined for dangerous driving. In the previous century James Tytler was even worse treated, though his achievements were notable in many directions, especially upwards, for he was the first man in Britain to ascend in a balloon. This he did in a hot-air balloon of his own construction in 1784 from Meadowbank, near the site of the present Sports Stadium.

He also discovered a cheap way of manufacturing magnesia, wrote most of the 2nd edition of the Encyclopaedia Britannica (though that massive publication cannot find any space to mention him now); He wrote the song, "The Muckin' o' Geordie's Byre" (which for the benefit of English hearers, can also be sung as "The Cleansing of George's Cowshed); not yet weary of practical work, he also did some personal research, and composed and printed "A list of the Ladies of Pleasure in Edinburgh", which is unhappily a little out of date.

He was tried for sedition, not pornography, but fled the country or "fugitated", which the Scots Magazine unkindly mis-spelt as "fumigated" a method of ridding a house of plague or vermin. Burns knew him well and described his style of headgear as "a sky-lighted hat."

In theology one would have expected sublime and harmonious expressions to be used but the fanatics had a store of uncouth phrases to bring Heaven down to Earth with a thud. One theological treatise had as a sub-title "A loupin-on stane for heavy-arsed believers," which perhaps inspired the proverb about the pious,

"They wad flee if their erses wad let them."

Even girls in love could not forget the practical things in life. There is a lovely lyric sung by a love-sick lass extolling the merits of her four sweethearts but the last couplet of each verse ends similarly to this

"But then alas he is sae puir
He winna dae for me."

The Scots also have a down-to-earth proverb on love without lolly.

"It's lang or four bare legs gaither heat in a bed."

Even the dead were not allowed to rest in peace away from this atmosphere of utility. An Edinburgh merchant blessed with a loving wife was not content to leave her to God's mercy but recorded this ludicrous epitaph.

"Here lies inter'd her Corps in hopes to rise
Whose soul's above with Christ in Paradise.

Not Gadie, kept her shop, went not abroad
Virtuous and charitable serving God.

110

When the phrenologists were in full swing about a century and a half ago they had the human head portioned off into allotments for twenty or more different faculties such as amativeness, aggressiveness, philoprogenitiveness and such "lang-nebbit" words. Poor Burns' skull was exhumed in 1834 and awarded marks out of twenty for each of these characteristics. Surprisingly he did not gain full marks for amativeness, though he did quite well for poetic ability.

Burke, the multi-murderer, appears, in the main, to have had almost as good a score as Burns. Apart from the trifling matter of a few suffocations, we might have had Burke Suppers and Immoral Memories.

When James the Fat, 4th Earl of Douglas, died, he had to satisfy the practical men who have left us the gruesome record of this aristocratic gluttonous lie-a-bed.

"The 25th March 1443 Earl James Douglas died at the Castle of Abercorn. The cause of death was his having in his guts more than four stones of tallow."

One is led to surmise who the ghouls were that conducted the P.M. Were they butchers, bakers or candle-stick makers? Or was it just idle curiosity that had to be satisfied?

The wind, in the best sense, was the inspirer of poets. For that reason pigs, which can forecast wind by squealing, were beasts sacred to the muse of poetry. Medically, the wind is not of such a high order, and is a term rather loosely applied.

The bright young thing, given to the slang of the Twenties, said to the old wifie, "I fairly got the wind up," to which the old-fashioned lady replied, "Eh, that must hae been an awfu relief."

In a country kirk an old lady sat near the door and the minister, anxious for her well-being, and knowing the kirk to be draughty, asked her if she was not troubled with the wind, to which she replied, "O, aye, gey often, but I tak care no to brek it till the organ starts."

In districts where plumbing was in the future, pails were a godsend, so a country woman shopping in Edinburgh bought one in Woolworth's and made for the bus-stop. She had some time to wait so she sat on the pail. To a newsboy who called out, "Paper, missus?" she replied, "Na, ye impident chiel, I'm just waitin' for the Peebles bus."

Even in the grave moments of birth and death, practical matters had to be considered.

An absolutely true incident in the life of a border doctor.

He went miles up a glen to deliver a shepherd's wife. Ben the hoose, after a long labour, he successfully brought a fine pair of twin boys into that upland world. He went back to the fireside where the herd was sitting.

"Well, Jock, I'm delighted to inform you that your wife has presented you with a fine pair of boys."

"Ma Goad," exclaimed Jock, "And the coo's dry."

111

The old laird lay dying, but, as he had been doing this for a couple of years, his housekeeper took the situation quite calmly. One evening he began to groan again.

"O, Jeanie, I'm shair ma end is near this time. In fact this vera nicht the Lord will require my soul. I feel certain o't."

"Weel, laird," replied Jeanie, very sympathetically. "I'm vera sorry for ye, but if it's to be as you say, it wad be vera convenient, for the coo's gaun tae calf, and I've nae time to attend to ye baith."

In the face of disaster, when everyone was panicking the practical Scot was able to "keep the heid" and make the best of it.

The old Scots sailor was telling about his experiences during storms at sea.

"I mind I was on a ferry-boat full of passengers when a terrible squall blew up. We could mak nae headway and the waves were brakin' ower the bulwarks. The folk began to cry out for somebody to pray for the storm to die doon. The captain said to me, 'You're a God-fearing man. Get up a prayer'. But I said I couldna pray; neither could I say a psalm. So he said, 'Then for ony sake dae something religious.' Sae I whipped aff ma bannet and took up a collection."

Here is a story about a hypothetical birth which, as far as the records go, never came to be anything more.

Scots sometimes take chances but they prefer to bet on a certainty. An old age pensioner thought he had done the right thing when he told his pensioner bride that he had provided her with a fine wee flat, nine storeys up in the Lawnmarket of Edinburgh. But she surprised him when to his dismay she exclaimed, "Aye, John, it's no a bad wee hoose and has a grand view o' the sea but I've never seen sic an awkward stair for a pram."

The cottagers of East Berwickshire (called "The Merse) pretended for their own purposes that they had a good and sufficient economical reason for shifting to another employer, though all they really wanted was a change of district. But they had to give the farmer a better reason than just "a change of air." One flimsy excuse was that they wanted a little more grass for the hens. The proverb arose:

For a hen's gerss
They'll flit in the Merse.

The craze for precision was carried into everything. Probably the parterre gardens favoured by the French and Dutch, and brought into Britain also were a reflection of the excessive love of law and order which led to the reaction of the French Revolution. Paul Jones (or John Paul), the father of the American navy, was, as a boy, a victim of this formalism. His father was gardener to old Earl Douglas at St Mary's Isle on the Solway. The Earl was fanatical about symmetry and inspected the gardens each day looking for flaws. He spied a disconsolate boy looking through the window of a summerhouse and was told that he had been caught stealing apples. From the matching summerhouse the face of an equally tearful boy was peering. The gardener was questioned.

"Oh, that's my ain laddie. I pit him in for symmetry."

Boys in olden times were often very ill-used, especially by burghs which held Common Ridings. It was the custom, at each landmark on the boundary, to whip the boys on the bare buttocks with birch rods or other weapons, so that they would remember the place all their lives. As Carlyle said of the schoolmasters of his day, "Of the human soul they know this much, that it has a faculty called memory, which can be acted upon through the application of birch rods to the muscular integument."

Poets are not expected to be very practical folk, though they often are. Sometimes a sharp experience of reality brings them to their senses.

Thomas Campbell, the poet, when a young man, was on a walking tour in the South of Scotland. A spell of stormy weather drove him to put up at a small inn on Tweedside. After a good supper, followed by toddy, he lay in bed happily musing on a poetic theme.

There was a soft tap at his door and the dainty serving-lass, shading a candle, crept in.

She smiled shyly. "Sir, could ye tak a neebour into your bed?"

"With all my heart," breathed the young poet, moving briskly over.

"Thank ye, sir," said the lass, "for Johnny Grizzel, the Moffat carrier has just come in soaked to the skin."

Shortly after, Campbell's famous poem was published, "The Pleasures of Hope."

A minister who took an interest in all his parishioners noticed a great number of small children belonging to unmarried mothers. When asked who the father was, many young women would not tell.

"What colour of hair had he, then?"

"I dinna ken. He never took his bunnet aff."

But at last he discovered the identity of the womaniser, and went to see him. He started on an ingratiating note.

"How d'ye get round all these women?"

"Ach, it's nae bother. I hae a bicycle."

A Lothian farmer was notorious for his procreative powers on both sides of the blanket but he was not a man to offend, so nobody remonstrated with him during his long life. But when his massive tombstone came to be made, the mason was able to make an enduring comment on it, registering the general disapproval, by using italics for the operative word.

HERE LYES JOHN SPOUSE FARMER IN MOUNT PROGENY DYED 11th OCTOBER 1874 AGED 86.
WHO HAD 41 *LEGITIMATE* CHILDREN BY HIS TWO WIVES . . .

In religious matters people were not allowed to forget the practical side.

Half-crowns were pleasant possessions for the poor, but they caused serious disasters; they were often mistaken for pennies.

When the ladle came round one Sunday, Jock carelessly threw in his penny, as he thought. To his horror it was a half-crown but he could not retrieve it. However he allowed the ladle to pass Sunday after Sunday. On the thirtieth Sabbath the officiating elder held the ladle before him firmly, and whispered, "Your time is up, Jock."

There is a rather unlikely tale of six Scottish mourners who hired a cab to take them to a burial a couple of miles away. The cabbie said he wouldn't charge any definite fare but would make a bargain. Every word they spoke would cost them a shilling. He drove them furiously over the rough surface to make them cry out, but not a word came. At the kirkyard he opened the door and all six got out, very hot and exhausted.

"You never uttered a word," said the cabbie.

"Maybe no," said one, "but we were gey near it when the bottom fell oot o' the cab aboot a mile back."

A servant lass from the Covenanting country was working in a large farm on the east coast. She carelessly dropped a pile of crockery on the stone floor and, when the irate mistress came hurrying up, the maid smugly assured her that this accident "maun just hae been predestined to happen."

This was more than flesh and blood could stand, so the mistress gave her a resounding "daud on the chafts," which sent her across the room, retorting at the same time, "Predestined to happen! Weel, and sae was that."

An English bishop was on holiday in the Scottish borders. He got into conversation with a shepherd.

"How many sheep are in your charge, my friend?"

"Exactly forty-twa score."

"Now let me see. That is eight hundred and forty."

"Aye, I think that'll be aboot richt."

"Do you know, my good friend, that I have a flock of fifty thousand? What do you think about that?"

"I'm thinking', if what ye say is true, that ye maun hae a hell o' a job at lambin' time."

Shepherds know their business, and only fools rush in to tell them how to manage it.

A business man in a Southern city had purchased a sheep-farm and wisely left the running of it to a manager. In the spring the business tycoon heard a rumour that wool prices were about to rise, so he telegramed his manager,

"Start clipping."

Back came a wire. "Can't clip. Lambing."

This brought the reply. "Stop lambing, start clipping."

When Scots and Jews go into partnership they tend to suffer from eye-strain before long. One of these very successful business Scots, a Fifer, was the envy of an English friend who asked him the secret of his success.

"It's a matter of brain feeding. I'll tell ye what I'll dae. I'll send ye some brain feeding twice a month and at the end of six months you'll find a distinct improvement. The cost will be £1 a lesson."

Each fortnight the Scot sent off a pair of Arbroath smokies to the South. At that time this cost him half-a-crown for which he received £1 by return. After three months his English pupil enclosed a note with his postal order.

"Don't you think £1 is rather dear for two smoked fish?"

The Fife man wrote back, "Recommend you continue course. Undoubtedly beginning to show results."

Small shopkeepers have a hard job nowadays, but they always had to be shrewd and practical to make ends meet. They never had to allow stock to run low. A "Jenny A'thing", or woman keeping a general store, had married five times and lost all five husbands. She was asked one day, shortly after her latest bereavement, how her husband was.

"Weel, I'm awfu' sorry, but I'm oot o' men the noo."

"Willie A'thing" in Galashiels boasted that he stocked everything, so a local wag went in and asked him for a pair of handcuffs. He got the imperturbable Willie's reply.

"I'm oot o handcuffs the-day, but I'll get a few pairs by the Embro carrier the morn."

The organiser of the Edinburgh evening classes assured the public that he had classes for all trades and professions. A wag came up to his office. "What course is it you want, my young man?" "I want yin for lion-tamers." "That's a cultural class. We need only twelve students to start it. Come up tomorrow with eleven of your friends and we'll start you right away."

The Scots, like the Hollanders, hate to see anything wasted.

When Edinburgh employed horse-drawn water-carts to sprinkle the dusty dungy streets, an old country wife stopped the driver and said to him.

"Hoots, man, ye careless loon, div ye no see ye're skailin' a' the waitter?"

In Aberdeen even the horses were affected by the spirit of thrift. A Clydesdale held up the traffic in Union Street and, as it weighed about a ton, it was hard to shift. Nobody knew why it had taken such a "sturdy" turn. At last it began to tap the ground with its right fore-foot, so its driver, thinking it was hurt, lifted up the hoof and found the cause of the trouble—a threepenny bit which it was covering.

Here are three amusing but untrue stories from "Aiberdeen awa."

Auld Sandy looks in to commiserate with the newly bereaved widow.

"I'm real sorry to hear that peer Jeemie has gane."

"O, aye, he laid by his beets and took to his bed and ne'er raise."

Sandy sits for a while, deep in mournful thought.

"Did the corp happen to meention a wee pottie o' reid leid afore he slippet awa?"

The neighbour pops his head in and finds Andra stripping off the wallpaper.

"Renovatin'?"

"Na, flittin'."

The ticket inspector came round the crowded compartment train and everyone in Jock Macdonald's carriage presented their tickets, except Jock. He fumbled in all his pockets without success. The inspector waited impatiently and then saying he would be back shortly, he went out.

A gentleman turned to Jock; "I say, I know where your ticket is. I saw you slip it into your mouth just before the inspector came in."

"Wheesht, man," said Jock, "I ken. I was just sookin' aff the date."

A snuff addict saw a fine figure of a man in full tartan regalia standing on the steps of a hotel. His nose was aquiline and his nostrils very wide. He looked the very embodiment of Celtic pride of race. The snuffer went up to him and proffered his snuff-box. The grandee inclined his head imperceptibly and replied with cold formality:

"Thank you, I never take it."

The snuffer was not in the least put out. He took a pinch himself and remarked:

"Man, that's an awfu peety, for ye've grand accommodation."

The chief fault one can find with practical people is that, like the Man with the muck-rake in the Pilgrim's Progress, they cannot see the glorious opportunities, and the marvels of the universe, for peering into the trifling commonplaces of existence.

A centenarian dame of the old Scots school was told she must have witnessed many changes in her time from John Knox's days until the days of James Graham, "Bonnie Dundee," the well-known persecutor of the Covenanters.

"Hoots, awa, no that mony changes. When I was a lassie Knox was deivin' folk wi his clavers, and noo, when I'm auld, Claver'se is deivin' folk wi' his knocks."

In the days when the coaches, named after important gentry, plied between Aberdeen and Fochabers, notices of the times of departure and arrival were displayed in public places. In Fochabers, which was then a small village near the palace of the Duke of Richmond and Gordon, the following prominent notice was long displayed without raising the slightest blush or cry of protest.

"God willing, the Duchess of Gordon will leave the Duke's Arms punctually each morning at nine o'clock, except the Sabbath."

The mysteries of space were beyond the scope of many simple folk so they applied practical common sense to this subject, with ridiculous results.

A dear old lady praised Sir Isaac Newton like this:

"Sir Isaac Newton was as weel acqueent wi the stars as if he had been born and brocht up amang them."

A country wench, visiting Perth for the first time, was not aware of the custom of firing a gun at sunset. She jumped at the sudden report.

"What was that?"

"Oh, that's just the sunset."

"Losh me, I've seen it gang doon hunners o' times, but that's the first time I've kent it to gang doon wi' sic a muckle dunt."

There seems to be very little room for romance in some Scots, when they can make a financial gain.

"I got the chance o' a lifetime last week" said the young Glaswegian "An' I took it. I was walking along the Great Western when a Jag drew up, and the smashin' dame drivin' it asked me if I wantet a lift. She drove me up a quiet country road near Balloch, stopped, and stripped aff to the buff.

'Now, you can have what you like,' says she."

"What did you do?" eagerly asked his listeners.

"Ach, I took the Jag, her claes widna hae fittit me onywey."

The love of money is the root of evil and Scots, admittedly, are not free from this vice. An avaricious Scot had died and his friends were discussing his affairs.

"They are saying," said one, "that John left twenty thoosand pund."

"They're saying what's no true, then," retorted another, "It wad be mair true to say he was ta'en awa frae it."

Before the Reformation the Abbot of Dunfermline, who owned the Ferry Passage, told an agent to form a joint stock company to sell off the Ferry rights as profitably as possible. The agent divided them into sixteen shares and sold eighteen of them. This was the first joint-stock company in Britain. Sharp practice is not a new art.

A mill-hand got a guinea a week wages. The first pay-day he gave his wife a sovereign and kept the bob. The second week he gave her the bob and kept the sovereign. She turned on him. "Hoo d'ye think I'm gaun tae manage on that?" "I dinna ken," said he, "I had a hell o' a job last week."

Despite its situation in a fertile part of Nithsdale there must have been extreme poverty or thrift in Kirkmahoe parish. The 'gustin' bane o' Kirkmahoe' became proverbial. Bones were purchased in Dumfries and hired out to parishioners to flavour soup by being tied to a string and dipped three times and then whisked round the pot. This cost a halfpenny. The bone then went on to the next hirer.
A rhyme was made up,
  "Wha'll buy me? Wha'll buy me?
  Three plumps and a wallop for a bawbee."
This, when chanted in the presence of Kirkmahoe men, started a riot.

To hear that someone had "ta'en to their bed," was pretty serious, as it meant either a birth or a death, so when an elderly country doctor got word on a wild wet morning that a young woman in an upland farm had "Ta'en to her bed" he set off to see what he could do. He found the servant-lass in her room, apparently in the best of health. He could find no signs of illness, nor of pregnancy. At last she confided, "They've ne'er paid me a penny-piece o' wages for three months so I'm bidin' here until they pay me."
"Lie aboot, lass," said the doctor. "That's a vera guid idea o' yours. I'm comin' in aside ye. They've no paid a bill o' mine for twa years."

Security is a key-word these days and it was a very important thing in any age. In lawless Scotland property was always at grave risk, so when the people of Jedburgh got the chance they found a solution.
Johnny Armstrong (not the famous outlaw but a common robber), was brought to Jedburgh for trial, which, here, often meant execution first and trial later, but Johnny was offered his freedom if he would tell the best way to defeat robbers. He answered "A terrier and a rusty key:" hence the rhyme.
  "A terrier tyke and a rusty key
  Were Johnny Armstrong's Jeddart fee."

The Scots of old were rough and ready no doubt, but nobody can question the practicability of their methods.
A remote householder was asked: "What happens when illness occurs?"
"There's ile for the beasts and whisky for the folks and them that dees, just dees," he replied, philosophically.

A minister set off to baptise a babe at the Back Hill o' the Bush in Kirkcudbrightshire but the burn was in spate and he could not get across. However the difficulty was overcome by the father holding the child over the stream while the minister splashed water upon it and shouted the words of the service above the roar of the torrent.

THE GREAT DIVIDE

The Great Divide in Scotland is usually taken to be the geological fault which runs roughly between Stonehaven and Helensburgh and separates the Highlands from the Lowlands. It was often called the Highland Line and in olden times it was a boundary to be respected, particularly by the Lowlanders, for a different race of folk, speaking a totally different language and observing a completely strange way of life, lived to the north-west of it. The Highlanders often crossed it, for various reasons; either to make a spreagh or cattle-raid, or to wage war, or latterly to sell their sheep and cattle in the great annual sales. As the years went on this line became less and less a Great Divide, and Scotland regained the unity which it had rejoiced in for most of the middle ages.

If variety is the spice of life, so is diversity, and Scotland can claim a large amount of it within its own small borders.

One of the lesser divides is a social one. Edinburgh gave birth to R. L. Stevenson and he embodied the contrasts of Edinburgh's people in "Dr Jekyll and Mr Hyde." Stevenson was brought up in a genteel circle in Edinburgh's New Town.

His heart was not in the legal business for which his family intended him, so he did not remain long in it. He seems to have frequented the lower quarters of the Old Town as a gay Bohemian. No greater contrast can be imagined than what he experienced. The fun began when one clashed with the other.

In the cable-car days, one of the routes ran from the elite Morningside to the equally select Goldenacre suburb. However it passed near the crowded rookeries of the Potterow and Bristo, before collecting passengers from the Law Courts, so a great social mix was made in the tramcar.

At that time, the poorer women wrapped their babies about them in tartan shawls, and fed them from the breast in public without self-consciousness.

One afternoon a very supercilious gentleman from the Law Courts got on at Parliament House and sat down facing a young Bristo mother and her infant. As the crowded car rattled down the Mound, the mother tried without success to interest the bairn in its drink. The solicitor pretended not to see her. Then in a shrill voice the mother scolded the sleepy child: "Come on noo, tak' it, tak' it. If ye dinna tak' it, I'll gie it to that nice mannie ower there."

The same area of Edinburgh saw many such clashes. A legal light was accosted by what Lord Braxfield called "a hure off the streets."

"How dare you approach me, woman," he said, "Are you not aware that I am a Crown Solicitor?"

"I'm no sae up in the warld as you, maybe. But we're baith at the same game, for I'm a hauf-crown solicitor."

Edinburgh has been pilloried enough as the city of Sin, Sun and Snobs; as "East-windy, West-endy;" as "that awfu place that ye've to gang up stairs to." (i.e. the Waverley Station Steps.) A native can be recognised anywhere by the habit he has of holding his hat on as he turns a corner; in the suburbs the natives eat kippers off the piano-tops (or used to, before the first became a luxury, and the second a drug on the market); where the "only sign of life was the smoke from the crematorium."

Let us now move to the country.

A tenants' dinner was being arranged by the laird. At this annual event, homespun rubbed elbows with silk and sparks were often generated.

Farmer Brown had never been at such an occasion, so he sought advice from a friend.

"Hoo would ye mak polite conversation?" asked Brown.

"Well, it's really very simple, even when speaking with strange ladies. You open by remarking on the weather, then you proceed to discuss dress, and if this goes satisfactorily you could indulge in a light flirtation."

Brown took careful note of these three points, and when he found himself seated next to a lady member of the country aristocracy, he began to put his trainer's advice to use.

He nudged the lady in the spare-ribs.

"It's fell guid weather for the neeps," he ventured. She looked puzzled but smiled, as if he were a foreigner. Brown was encouraged to pass to position two—dress.

"D'ye wear reid flannel next your skin?"

She blushed as if she suspected an undue intimacy.

Now was the time for a little flirtation, thought Brown, so he rattled his knuckles down her backbone as far as her backless dress would allow, and cried jocularly,

"Hey, wumman, are ye kittly?"

It could be said that the Celtic people invented nuclear fission over two thousand years ago, for no sooner had the nucleus of a community or clan been formed, than it began to split up. The Pictish people were divided into seven sub-kingdoms; the Gaels had a proverb "The clans of the Gaels, shoulder to shoulder," but history tells a different story; even the Angles were originally so anti-social that they avoided towns and built their homes out of sight of one another. So it is not to be wondered at that rivalries have always existed between communities in Scotland.

The Glasgow man says, "I'd raither be hanged in Glesca than dee a natural death in Paisley." They speak of the men of Glasgow, the folk of Greenock, and the bodies of Paisley.

In the north the Aberdonian says, "I'll draw a map of Scotland." He then makes a giant Z with a large dot on the tail and says "Aiberdeen. Fat's the gweed o' gaun ony farther."

A saying with the same message is "Tak awa' Aiberdeen and twal mile roon' and far are ye?"

Here in the North, we have the bodies of Angus, the men o' the Mearns, and the canny folk o' Aiberdeen.

The old wifie in the kirk had little need to pray, "O Lord, we beseech thee to grant that we may ay hae a guid conceit o' oorsels."

Aberdonians think advertising does no harm, though very few Scots in the south would understand this; "There's as gweed beets and sheen made in the auld toon o' Aiberdeen as in a' breed Skwytland."

The Highlanders finally ended the feuds involving bloodshed and rapine, but still kept the old fires smouldering. They thought in terms of clanship, rather than of any other association.

The tale is told of a traveller, nearly perishing in a terrible blizzard, who saw the lights of a clachan not far away. He struggled towards the door of the nearest house and banged upon it. The door was cautiously opened and a voice cried, "Who is that at this hour of night?"

"For God's sake, let me in. I'm at my last gasp with hunger and cold. Open the door and let me in, if you are Christians."

"Indeed, you'll just need to be ganging on then, for we don't know the Christians. We're a' Camerons here."

Here is one version of a well-known tale, intended to insult numbers of other clansmen.

A travelling menagerie passing over a bleak moorland had the misfortune to find that a monkey had died of a chill, so they threw it into a ditch.

Two shepherds came upon the corpse the following day and began to speculate on its identity.

"Indeed, Dugal, he might be a Cameron but he's ower straight in the nose."

"Surely that is so, Ian. But could he not be a Fraser?"

"Ach, no, he's too handsome."

"And I would think he was a Stewart, but his legs are too small and his nose is too short."

"Indeed that is so."

"Then I'm sure by the twist of his mouth that he's either a damned Campbell from Inverary or a visitor from the hotel in Oban."

A certain man of the great clan Campbell had an argument with a MacNeil as to which clan was the older. At the hottest point of the argument Campbell (locally pronounced Cam'ell) making a play of his name said that Noah had had a pair of camels in the ark. Could the MacNeils produce any evidence that they had formed part of Noah's crew?

Stumped for a moment the islandman at last snorted out, with concentrated pride of race, "Did ye not know then, that we would not be beholden to yon Noah, for the MacNeils had aye a boat of their own?"

Maxtone of Cultoquey was an eccentric laird whose estate was surrounded by four great landlords, any one of whom would have welcomed the chance of adding Maxtone's land to their own. He knew their natures very well, so, being a very forthright and courageous man, he determined to defy them and put his judgment of their characters to the test.

He invited them all, Campbell, Graham, Drummond and Murray, to dinner and intimated that he would say grace, which was:

"O, Lord, we ask thee to bless to us this repast and furthermore

From the pride of the Grahams
From the greed of the Campbells
From the wind of the Murrays
From the ire of the Drummonds

O, Lord, deliver us,
           Amen.

The dinner was not a social success.

Religious differences occasioned more conflict and bloodshed than any other: the smaller the differences in beliefs, the greater the antagonism. Many readers of Burns will have been puzzled by the expressions "Auld Lichts" and "New Lichts", and may have wondered wherein the difference lay. These were only the nicknames for two sub-sections of the Associated Synod, who both insisted on calling themselves the Associated Synod, in much the same way as the two Popes, during the times of the "Babylonian Exile" from Rome to Avignon, insisted that each was the real Pope and the other an imposter. The "Auld Lichts" refused to take the Burgher's Oath swearing to support Protestantism, while the "New Lichts" took the oath.

An old proverb sarcastically describes such nigglers, "Muckle to mak a wark aboot, a deid cat in your parritch."

I once heard an evangelist speaking at the Mound (the Edinburgh Forum in my youth), describing how he went into a West End church and was so stirred by the preaching of the worthy divine that he stood up in the gallery and shouted, "Hallelujah"; which of course caused a sensation and made the church officer come and tap him on the shoulder, and lead him outside with the severe rebuke, "We dinna dae that here."

It was different in Edinburgh in the earlier centuries when religious fervour shook the earth to its foundations and many a preacher was known to cry more than "Hallelujah".

One popular preacher was praised in this sentence, "Eh, he's a maist powerfu' preacher. D'ye ken, in the fower years sin' he cam', he's smashed twa pulpits and dung the guts oot o' fower Bibles."

One such enthusiast was always denouncing the "Scarlet Woman", the Whore of Babylon. Towards the end of his hour's sermon, observing that the glass had yet a little sand to run, he remarked to his congregation, "We hae just time to hae anither wap at the Red Lady."

So many Highlanders flocked into Auld Reekie (as well as into Glasgow) to seek employment as caddies, (i.e. messengers or porters) or sedan-chairmen, that a Gaelic Church was set up to the south of the Castle. The congregation was large and all the services were in Gaelic, the clergyman being the Rev. Joseph Robertson, who was renowned for his conviviality whether the occasion was a baptism, a wedding or a funeral. On the day when the Proscription Acts against the Macgregors were repealed, Robertson came out in his true clan colours. He paraded the streets dressed in a full suit of Macgregor tartan and at the head of his congregation of 1500 celebrated his restoration of rights far into the night. The City Guard (named by Robert Fergusson, the Black Banditti), being Highlanders to a man, there was no means of stopping this bacchanalian debauch, and no doubt, the great divide between the Lowlanders and Highlanders was temporarily filled up with usqueba.

The chief export of the Hebrides was, for a long time, ministers, soldiers and policemen, all of whom had a genius for "hauding the wretches in order." There was little love lost between them and the citizens of Glasgow and Edinburgh. In Edinburgh the City Guard with their Lochaber axes had been feared, and with good reason, for they used them freely. Fergusson says,

> "Jock Bell gaed furth to play his freaks
> Great cause he had to rue it
> For frae a stark Lochaber aix
> He gat a clamihewit (heavy blow)
> Fu' sair that nicht."

The Victorian police relied more on muscle to keep the law. As they were mostly Gaelic speakers, they were subject to much ridicule from the Glaswegians who had never quite got over the "Highland Host," who were let loose on the "Westland Whigs" in 1679; and the imposition put on the city by Prince Charlie in 1745.

A huge "polis" rolled up to a band of young men who were chatting one Sunday evening in Renfield Street. He gave the nearest a push and cried, "If you're going to be standing there, you'll need to be moving on."

There was a general guffaw at this and one of the lads retorted, heatedly, "Is this no a free country?"

The reply came with withering scorn.

"This iss no a country at aal, at aal, ye tamned eediot. This iss the biggest city in the hale toon o' Glasgow."

Hearing a scuffle up a close one night the 'polis' shone his lantern and called out:

"Hoo many are there o' ye in there?"

"Five."

"Far ower mony. Come oot the half o' ye."

A large Dalmatian dog was running loose in a public park, causing some annoyance to the public. The park-keeper called to a passing policeman for support in rounding it up.

The policeman addressed a number of citizens seated on benches by the path.

"Who iss it that's belonging to the pig white dog over yonder, that has a black spot every now and again?"

Members of Highland clans have given their name to objects that have benefited mankind. MacAdam devised a new method of making good roads. (A professor of comparative philology has pointed out that the word 're-macadamising' is derived from five languages in this order, Latin, Gaelic, Hebrew, Greek and English.)

MacIntosh invented a rubberised fabric; his name is synonymous with waterproof coat.

This has sometimes led to confusion and amusement.

The agitated tourist who had mislaid his raincoat ran up and down the platform where the Oban train was waiting to pull out, crying at each carriage window, "Is there a black macintosh in there?" He did not recover his property but the station-master had his own suspicions about where it had gone, for, from one carriage in reply to his question, there had come the answer, "Na, na, we're a' red Macgreegors in here;" a clan with a bad reputation for 'lifting'.

The same sort of mistake arose during a Highland Games in rather rainy weather. A sudden shower swept down from the bens and sent everyone scurrying for cover. A city gentleman had come unprovided against the West Highland climate, so he ran in some agitation seeking protection for himself and his lady wife.

He entered the competitors' tent, where many brawny Highland athletes were assembled and cried out,

"Could I have a macintosh to cover my wife?"

A red-headed mountaineer sprang forward eagerly:

"I'm no' a MacIntosh. I'm a MacPherson. Would I no do as weel?"

One of the clan chiefs is supposed to have had a rebuff when trying to enter a "Games" enclosure, reserved for V.I.P.s He protested loudly to the gatekeeper.

"Look here, my man, you have no business to keep me out. I am the MacIntosh of MacIntosh."

"I don't care if you're the Umbrella of Umbrella, you don't get in here without a ticket."

All these dissentions, rivalries and misunderstandings could be multiplied time and again. We should rejoice that after centuries of feuds the whole business is just a rather amusing memory.

Strange though it may seem, some wild men repented of their bad behaviour, however unwillingly.

On a Clyde steamer, an old lady had been asking rather too many obligations from one of the sailors, a West Highlandman. Finally he turned on her, "Ach, go to hell."

She went straight to the captain and complained of his rudeness, demanding an apology.

The captain went to him, "Dugal, you've to apologise to that lady for swearing at her."

"Well, she asked for it. She's just an old —."

"That's enough, Dugal. Now I'm ordering you to apologise."

Dugal very unwillingly approached the lady.

"Are you the woman I told to go to hell?"

"I am indeed."

"Well, the captain said I was to tell you there's no hurry."

Rob Roy decided he would go to Father Drummond at Drummond Castle and make confession of his sins. Nobody was eavesdropping near enough to hear all the irregularities he had confessed to, but Father Drummond was heard to groan loudly and seen to cross himself repeatedly and exact a heavy payment. Rob no doubt felt his account with the Almighty was squared and he could start afresh. He was heard to say that, as far as his case was concerned, absolution was a "sair waste o uilzie. (oil.)"

When on his death-bed he is well-known to have got himself rigged out in full Highland panoply of war to confront a visitor with whom he had long been at feud. He did not wish to show any sign of weakness.

This was the spirit in which a clansmen prayed for help from his Creator: "O, Lord, look after my friends. I'll look after my enemies mysel'."

The patriarch on his death-bed repented of his shortcomings to the minister and was urged to forgive all his enemies. He agreed, and his family gathered round to hear him.

"I forgie thae rascals the MacIntnachs wha robbed me o' twa kyloes, likewise the Camerons of Rannoch that reived me o' a score o' gimmers, forbye the Frasers that burnt doon my hoose seventeen year back. I forgie them freely."

Then turning to his two sons he said sternly, "Ian and Chairlie, ye've heard me name them. See that ye spare neither time nor effort efter I am gane to revenge the wrangs I hae suffert."

Another, on his presumed death-bed, forgave his enemy, but added, "If I recover, things are to be the same between us as they were before."

These were exceptions, like that boorish Highlander who thought that Dr Johnson's name was Johnston and asked him if he was a Johnston of Ardnamurchan or some Hebridean island. On the learned doctor replying he was neither, he was told, "Then you must be a bastard."

Burns wrote,
>When Death's dark stream I'm ferry o'er
>A time that surely shall come
>In Heaven itself I'll ask no more
>Than just a Hieland welcome.

No higher praise could be given to the Highlanders, especially from a Lowlander who never wore the kilt and did not speak Gaelic (though his eldest son was proficient in it). I can never understand why kilts are worn at Burns Suppers. In Burns' day, in Ayrshire, they were a completely outlandish dress.

Those who had no Gaelic should not have felt superior to the Gael struggling with a totally different language, for they would have made a poor figure in his mother tongue. However it was sometimes more than a lack of English that gave rise to amusement. In these two cases it was applied mathematics that was lacking.

"Have you found your sheep, Donal'?"

"Aye, I found them."

"Where were they?"

"There was three by itself, and one all together, and two mixed up with one of Fraser's."

The police sergeant in Glasgow had traced a thief to a cinema so he put two newly enrolled constables to guard the exits. The programme ended, the house emptied, but no sign of the suspect.

"Did ye no' watch the exits, then?" he fumed.

"Och, aye, we watched them closely. He must have got away by one of the entrances."

The Lowlanders, too, felt that when they were in the Highlands, they were in a strange country and had to make excuses for their land of origin.

The Highland sheriff was trying to find out the place of birth of a very canny witness from whom with great difficulty he had drawn out his name and occupation.

"Come away, my man, where do you come from?"

"Frae the Sooth Country."

"Cannot you be more precise? Which part of the South country?"

"Frae somewhere about the Clyde."

"Which particular town or village?"

Cornered, the poor fellow blustered out,

"I was born in Paisley but as shair as daith, your honour, I couldna help it."

We now come to the Great Divide which separates Scotland from the rest of the world. Strange though it seems, Galloway was always looked upon as a region apart. The phrase was common, "The Fremit Scots of Galloway:" this was probably because Galloway was a detached part of the Gaelic world, Gaelic being spoken in the hill districts there until the 18th century. Most of the place names in the Rhinns of Kells are Gaelic though some have been reduced to phonetic English by the map-makers.

The Gallovidians are a shrewd and hardy race with a subtlety of thought which they probably inherit from the old Strathclyde Welsh, whose blood ran in the veins of St Mungo, Merlin, and nearer our own time, the volatile Jane Welsh, wife of the Sage of Chelsea, Carlyle.

A patriarchal Galloway shepherd bet a visitor that he would show him seven kingdoms from the summit of the Cairnsmore of Carsphairn, a prominent hill above his house. The wager was a bottle of whisky, which should have made the visitor chary of making a bet.

On the hill-top, the weather being clear, the shepherd pointed out the landmarks.

"Yon blue hills ower the Irish Sea are the Mountains of Mourne in the auld Kingdom of Ulster. Yonner's the humphy back o' Snaefell in the auld Kingdom o' Man. To your left under a dark cloud is Snawdon in the auld kingdom o' Wales. And ower the Siller Solway are the blue fells o' Cumberland in England. A' aboot ye is the auld Kingdom o' Scotland."

"But that's only five, so you lose your bet."

"Haud on a wee," was the pawky remark. "Up in the blue lift aboon ye is the Kingdom of Heevin' and"—here he tapped his staff on a granite slab—doon there is the kingdom that waits for ill-mannered chiels that drink by theirsels. The Kingdom o' Hell. Noo, oot wi your bottle."

The Cheviots are a Great Divide, as the Romans realised when they established Hadrian's Wall behind them. An attempt was made by James VI to form a No-Man's Land at the Solway end of the border. This debateable land was a political vacuum, which Nature, in the form of the Grahams, Armstrongs and Elliots, abhorred so much that they filled it immediately and from this safe wilderness raided both Scotland and England impartially. But right up to the Union of the Crowns the Scots and English still continued to threaten one another across the border.

In 1596 Scott of Buccleuch crossed into England and boldly rescued Willie Armstrong (Kinmont Willie) from Carlisle Castle. The story forms the subject of the famous ballad. When Queen Elizabeth heard of the incident "she stormed not a little" and demanded of Scott "how he dared to do this deed?" to which he replied "Madam, what will a *man* not dare to do?" No wonder one of the Popes said, "The Scots are a cure for the English."

The Three Hundred Years' War finally petered out but Scots for long found themselves in a strange land when amongst the Saxons.

A lady from Edinburgh was shopping in a fashionable London drapers, a long time ago, and wished to buy a length of black and white check serge. In Scotland this was named the chess-board or dambrod pattern, so she asked the male assistant for a dambrod pattern. He brought a dark blue which she rejected; various other colours were brought, but no checks. She was now driven to the last resort of the misunderstood Scot. She enunciated her request in the broadest vowels, slowly, loudly, and with facial contortions. "I want a dambrod pattern." The young man then appeared with a long roll of crimson which he threw down before her exclaiming rather hotly, "There you are, madam, that's the damnedest broadest pattern in the whole damned shop."

A Kirkcudbrightshire man from New Galloway, which lay many miles from New Galloway Station (now no more), had to attend a relative's funeral in London. On arrival at King's Cross he was met by a cousin who said she would call a taxi, to which he responded by asking, "Is the toon far frae the station?"

A Scots girl finished her employment in London and bought a ticket for Edinburgh. She then discovered that the label had come off her trunk. She startled the clerk at the window of the luggage office by thrusting her pale face forward and asking, "Could ye gie me a plaister for my chest?"

The world outside Scotland has always been very well known to most Scots, as the old proverb indicates:

"A Scot, a craw and a Newcastle grindstane traivel a' the warld ower."

However there are naive souls in all countries who have little idea of anything beyond their parish boundaries.

At Peterhead, during the days of Halley's comet it was commonly rumoured that the world was to come to an end. A fishwife was worried about this, not so much on her own account, as for fear of the consequences to her sons and relatives.

"Eh, the warld's to end, and there's a' oor lads up at the Greenland fishin'. Fat on earth will they do when they come back an' fin' that there's nae warld left to come back to?"

A Peebles man went on a European tour, also visiting many celebrated scenes in Britain. At each world-famous building or scene of grandeur, whether St Peter's, or the Dolomites, or the Lakes of Killarney, he reiterated, "Aye, fair wunnerfu'. But man, ye should see the Tweed at Peebles Brig."

On arrival back at Peebles Station he had to cross the Brig to reach his home. He paused, set down his bag and leant over the parapet. After a long pause he sighed and sadly murmured, "Eh, man, whit a bloody lee."

Some Scots believed in shutting their eyes to the natural grandeur, like the Highlander whose croft was in a fine situation, overlooking a vista of wood, fell and flood.

"What a marvellous scene to have before you, sunrise to sunset, through all the changing seasons," breathed a poetic visitor.

"Ach, maybe that iss so," he admitted, "But ye canna fatten coos on it."

A man of a completely different character was encountered by a band of bus tourists on the road near his cottage in the Borders.

"Can you tell us where we can go to have a view of distant hills and a wide panorama of the Borderland?"

"Weel, it's gey far on intae the gloamin' ", he said, "or I wad direct ye tae the tap o' the road overlooking the Tweed. But, d'ye ken, frae this hillside ye can get as far a view as frae Ben Nevis."

"Ridiculous. How can that be?" exclaimed one.

"Why don't you tell us the view is as far as from Mont Blanc?"

"Aye, just as far. Bide for half-an-'oor and I'll prove it."

Consumed with curiosity they waited.

"Noo," he proclaimed," just turn aboot and ye'll see the full moon risin' aboon the moor. That's near a quarter o' a million miles awa'. Can your Mong Blong dae better than that?"

Warming pans of brass, copper, or porcelain were used in great houses but the humbler folk used less valuable objects. Often, a maid was sent to warm the bed. But a hot stone wrapped in a woollen cloth, or an earthenware bottle filled with hot water was common. The general Scots name for all crockery was piggery. A pig was an earthenware bottle.

An English lady visitor was asked by her landlady if she would like a pig in the bed.

"Why on earth should I want a pig in my bed?"

"O, just to warm it up for ye. We a' do that here."

"Don't you find it sometimes makes a mess of the bed?"

"Na, we aye tak care to stuff up its moo wi' a cork."

The impatience of foreign visitors with the Scottish weather has always been an irritant to the natives.

An Englishman in a quiet Fife village couldn't get his golf because of the rain. He asked a canny old lad, "What in heaven's name do you do here when it rains?" The Fifer replied quietly, "We dinna interfere."

During the Napoleonic Wars a patriotic lady was arguing with a theologian on the value of prayer as an aid to victory. Her opponent assured her that the French would be praying to God for victory just as fervently as the Scots or English.

127

She thought about this for a moment or two, then snorted with scorn,
"The French pray! Nae doot they micht; but, jabberin' craturs, wha wad listen
to them?"

Many British people are alarmed, as they have always been, at the prospect of
foreigners, or coloured folk, taking over the country. One of these worried ladies
was having a holiday in a quiet Border district, which specialised in black-faced
sheep. She picked up the local paper and began to read the column "Situations
Vacant."

"My goodness" she exclaimed", "Thae furriners are fairly takin' ower wi' a
vengeance. Listen to the encouragement they're gettin' even frae oor ain Border
lassies."

"Read it oot, then," said the farmer, incredulously.

She read it loudly. "Wanted urgently, two blackfaced shepherds for May."

The Scots have little need to be alarmed at foreigners taking over, because
many parts of Scotland were quite alien to one another for centuries.

James VI, twitted by the English courtiers on the general poverty and
smallness of the Scottish towns, is said to have replied (referring to Nairn)
"There's a toon in the far North o' my dominions that's sae muckle in extent that
the folk in the west o't speak a different tongue frae the folk in the east o't, and
the tane disna understand a single word that the tither says."

In the west end of Nairn the Gaelic-speaking world began, and continued to
Inverness and beyond to the farthest Hebrides; in the east end English was
spoken.

Even within a few miles of England a visitor from either North or South would
find it impossible to understand the language.

Jedburgh, like Hawick, has a dialect all its own and a story is told of a
commercial traveller who asked if Chinese labour was being used in the railway
station, for he had just overhead two porters arguing as they struggled to get a
trolley through a doorway.

Said one "Yow pow min." (You pull, man.)

Replied his mate, "Pow yow min." (Pull you, man.)

THE THISTLE

The thistle was adopted as the emblem of Scotland at a very remote date. The legend is that in 990, when an army of Danes was sweeping across Strathmore, burning and ravaging the countryside, Kenneth III King of Scotland advanced with a makeshift army at short notice from Stirling towards Perth, which was in imminent danger. Kenneth marched to Luncarthy, four miles north of Perth and there took up a commanding position.

The next day the battle began, the Danes attacking with ferocity. For a long time, as at Bannockburn, the issue was in doubt, until the intervention of a band of countrymen, led by a ploughman named Hay and his sons. The Danes, thinking this to be a fresh army, broke and fled.

The Scots army had nearly been surprised and routed on the eve of battle by a night attack from the Danish camp, but the Danes, who were presumably barefoot as well as baresark, happened to cross a patch of *onopordon acanthium,* or Scottish thistles, and their cries of discomfort alerted the Scots sentries. This particular prickly plant, in preference to the many kinds of thistles found in Scotland, was then adopted as the national emblem and, not long after, found its way into the royal insignia.

The Scots Thistle is a handsome plant and suitable for the basis of a heraldic design but its chief merit, or demerit, depending on how you look at it, is its prickliness. The spines are penetrating and difficult to remove. "Nemo me impune lacessit" (Let no one approach me with impunity) is a favourite motto in

Scots tradition. The Borderers translate this as "Wha dare meddle wi' me?" As it says in the ballad of Kinmont Willie,

> "Now sound out trumpets, quo' Buccleuch,
> Let's waken Lord Scroope right merrilie,
> Then loud the Warden's trumpet blew
> 'O wha dare meddle wi me?'"

Robert Burns says he always spared the Scots Thistle when shearing weeds: his compassion would not be shared by most farmers, who look on it as a most obnoxious weed because of its ability to spread. Thistles were introduced by accident to North America where the creeping or Russian thistle, when withered and rolled by the wind, forms the famous tumbleweed of the prairies.

In several respects the Scots Thistle emblifies the Scots. They have the ability to take root in any part of the world, they are quick to resent any meddling or insult, and their humour is as deceptive as thistledown, for, despite its apparent innocence, it usually carries a seed of a penetrating nature. They flourish on any kind of ground, rich or poor.

In my schooldays there was a famous advertisement showing an old man removing thorns from a boy's naked foot, with the patriotic caption, "Ye maunna stramp on a thistle, laddie."

A humorous parody of Scripture was "Happy is the man that sitteth upon a thistle, for verily I say unto you, he shall rise again."

All Scots heroes have shared this thistle-like quality, sometimes to excess: but considering the nature of the opposition and the harsh age they lived in, it was all necessary for survival—Sir William Wallace, Sir Robert Bruce, Rob Roy or Robert Macgregor and Sir Robert Burns. Burns was knighted; the fact is well established.

In Currie's Life of Burns we read that when Burns visited an ancient Jacobite lady, Mrs Bruce of Clackmannan, who was a descendant of King Robert Bruce, she knighted the poet with a sword that had belonged to the king, remarking as she did so, that "She had a better right to do so than *some folk,*" meaning the house of Hanover.

Sir Robert Burns, like the others, had his full share of "pepper in his nose," and it is to this explosive quality that we owe the pugnacious "Scots Wha Hae."

Burns had got a soaking in riding to Gatehouse of Fleet and the hotel-porter had burnt his good riding boots while drying them. He rode apart from his companions in an ill-humour all the next day over the bleak moors, the words of "Scots Wha Hae" being hammered out while hot in his mind. In the evening he wrote them down. We can still feel the jag of the thistle in them.

It was in a similar humour that he wrote "Such a parcel of rogues in a nation," referring to the bribery and cajolery that led to the signing of the Treaty of Union in 1707.

> "We're bought and sold for English gold;
> Such a parcel of rogues in a nation."

At the Union, Lord Seafield, the Chancellor, who had been the leading figure in the agreement, objected to his brother, Colonel Ogilvie, dealing in cattle. He said that it was quite unbecoming to the status of the family to have a member in such a low trade. Colonel Ogilvie turned the tables neatly. "Tak' your ain tale hame. I sell nowt, but ye sell nations." When a brother could speak so plain, it showed how the Union rankled, and still does, as some of the following stories show.

130

Just before a general election, the largest grocery store in a country town was a social centre where all kinds of political arguments were heard. A commercial traveller, who was not one to argue with his bread and butter, was interviewing the manager and agreeing with his political views, which were conservative. The traveller noticed a message-boy passing with a basket of new-born kittens which he was taking down to the warehouse.

"Where are you taking these, my lad?" he asked.

"Doon to their mither in the cellar. She's to feed them."

"What party are they voting for?" was the jocular query.

"O, they're a' true blue tories," said the lad.

This reply surprised the manager, for the boy's father was an ardent nationalist.

The following month the traveller was in for his order and seeing the boy asked him how his conservative kittens were getting on.

"O, they're a' Scottish Nationalists noo," said the lad.

"How can that be? They were tories a month ago."

"Aye, so they were. But their een are open noo."

Not all Scottish battles were fought against Englishmen: many were between clans or rival factions in civil wars. But several major battles were fought between English and Scots. The east coast was a veritable cockpit, for that was the normal invasion route of the "Auld Enemy." The Scots were defeated at Flodden, Halidon Hill, the two battles of Dunbar, Pinkie, and the first battle of Falkirk; the English lost the three battles of Roslin, Bannockburn, Stirling Bridge and Nechtan's Mere near Forfar; so the score is pretty even. But Bannockburn is a name that fires all ardent Scots hearts, for it coincides with the triumph of Robert Bruce (whose equestrian statue now dominates the area), and also the reassertion of Scottish nationhood.

Small boys in Scotland used to celebrate Bruce's personal triumph in a rude rhyming chant:

"Bruce and de Boon were fechtin for the croon
Bruce took his battle-axe and knocked the buggar doon."

When a subscription was being made to pay Mr Pilkington Jackson for the statue of Bruce, a collector called at the house of my cousin, Miss Bone, or Bohun, and was rather taken aback when she got the joking reply, "Do you think it likely that I'm going to subscribe for a statue to the man who killed my ancestor?"

A party of English tourists was being shown over the field of Bannockburn by a local guide. He went into great detail about the phases of the battle, the large booty and the importance of the victory for Scottish independence. At the end of the visit as the party made for their buses they dipped into their pockets and proferred some gratuities. To their surprise the guide held up his hand in refusal, "Na, na," said he, "Pit up your siller. It's cost ye eneuch a'ready."

Wallace was a knight of good Strathclyde stock, so understandably he got very little support from the Norman factions, the Bruces, Comyns, De Quinceys, D'Umphravilles etc. He was for centuries the hero of the ordinary folk and his exploits, put into verse by Blind Harry, were for long the favourite reading in Scots households. "The Acts and Deeds of Sir William Wallace" was founded on a Latin version of Wallace's Life. written by his schoolmate John Blair, so its main incidents are by no means mythical, though many of the deeds attributed to him are possibly fiction. The poem was bound in calfskin and looked very like the Bible, from the outside.

The minister called one Sabbath evening on a patriotic Scots lady and found her engrossed in a well-thumbed volume which he presumed was the Scriptures.

"Ah, my dear lady, how delighted I am to find you reading the life of our saviour."

"Aye, meenister, mony's the nicht efter I gang to bed I lie in the silent 'oors and think o' naething else."

"Such devotion is admirable. And what do you think was the most wonderful episode in our saviour's life?"

"Weel, there were mony. But to my mind the grandest o' a' was on yon frosty mornin' when he soomed the Carron Water wi' his broadsword on his back and his dirk atween his teeth."

National or racial nicknames are in the very worst taste. A person should be addressed by his or her Christian or family name. To call Irishmen Paddy, Welshmen Taffy, Scotsmen Jock or Englishmen Tommy is to invite resentment.

A Cockney motorist in the Borders drew up close to a shepherd and called out,
    "Wot's the wye to 'Awick, Jock?"
The shepherd eyed him grimly for a minute.
    "I'm in a 'ell of a 'urry, Jock," urged the tourist.
    "Hoo did ye ken my name was Jock?" asked the herd.
    "Ow, I just guessed it."
    "Weel, seein' you're sae damned guid at guessin', ye can guess your way to Hawick," and rising and whistling up his dogs he stalked off into the "vacant wine-red moor."

A visitor from the south was on a conducted tour round the Trossachs. He was rather niggardly in his praise of the scenic beauties; the only phrase of commendation he uttered was one that would have been better left unspoken. That was when at Loch Katrine he remarked, "This beats Drury Lane all to sticks." But for the rest, Ben Lomond, Loch Ard, he had nothing but odious comparisons with England's beauties which Byron thought "tame and domestic."

At length, when they reached the shores of Loch Lomond, the guide had had enough. He cut a straw from a neighbouring patch of oats. He handed it to the southerner.

"What's this for, Jock?"

"For a refreshment. If ye can sook as well as ye can blaw, Loch Lomond's yours."

Dr Johnson pretended to be very severe on Scots, though he was too good a Tory to have anything but admiration for the Highland support of the Jacobite cause. His definition of oats is famous, "Food for men in Scotland, and horses in England." But he personally was not above enjoying a good dish of haggis, the main constituent of which is oatmeal.

He was making inroads on a large haggis, at dinner with a patriotic Scots family. The lady of the house asked him how he liked it.

"Very good for hogs, I believe," he grunted, not very graciously.

"Then pray," said she sweetly, "let me help you to some more."

A patriotic English lady, preparing to make sheep's head broth, called on the local butcher and when her turn came she spoke out loudly in the crowded shop.

"I wish to buy a sheep's head. I want a good one. In fact, make sure it is an English sheep's head."

The butcher called to the back shop.

"Jimmy, a sheep's heid for this leddy. And ca' the brains oot o' it."

Scots all claim some sort of descent from famous characters of ancient times. A Highlandman was fond of reciting his long lineage from a remote hero who lived about as far back as that Macpherson famous in the ballad;

"Phairson had a son
That married Noah's daughter,
Nearly spoilt the Flood
By drinking all the water."

One day the man of long descent was driving a sow along the road when he met a London gentleman who had been bored by his long ancestry, night after night, in the local hotel bar.

"Ah, Macpherson. That's a fine white pig you have. That'll be one of those famous ancestors of yours."

"Not at all, sir. She's nae relation o' mine. Just an acquaintance like yoursel'."

An evangelist was describing his campaign against Satan.

"Last month I was fighting the devil in Wick. Not long ago I was fighting the devil in Inverness. Three weeks ago I fought him in Dundee. Last week I was waging a war with him in Stirling. Tonight, beloved brethren, I am face to face with him in Falkirk and tomorrow I shall continue the fight in Haddington."

"That's the stuff," shouted an enthusiast from the back of the hall, "Keep drivin' the bugger sooth."

The English language was principally introduced into Scotland through "King James' Bible", which in turn resulted in the English version of the psalms and paraphrases. Before this time Acts of Parliament and all documents were written in Scots, which was a direct descendant of Anglo-Saxon. It would read like a foreign language today, and indeed the very look of it would turn the ordinary Scot against it. This is sad, but it must be admitted.

However, in olden time, the favourite reading by all classes, was in Scots, particularly "Wallace," "Bruce," and the rumbustious works of Sir David Lindsay whose principal satire was "The Three Estates." An elderly Scottish gentleman, bed-ridden, was too blind to read, and had friends to read passages to him. One of them thought it would be good for the old man's soul if he read to him passages from the Scriptures. He had got well into the story of the prodigal son when something outlandish in the language and the subject irritated the old man.

"Hoots awa, man, pit that Englisher's book awa and read me a bit oot o' Davie Lindsay. Yon's naething but a made-up story."

A Scot got into an argument with an Englishman about the relative sizes of their countries. The Scot was sure that Scotland was bigger than England. He went to some length to point out how many miles of coastline there were in Scotland, compared with England. At last an atlas was produced giving the areas of each country in the British Isles. He had to admit that England had nearly double the area of Scotland, but he saved his face by having the last word.

"I'll admit Scotland is sma'er than England, but when ye think hoo mony mountains we hae, ye maun admit we wad be bigger than England gin oor country was a' rowed oot."

There were many Scots, Irish and Welsh in the British navy. Scots had a great naval tradition. John Paul, or Paul Jones as he later named himself, the father of the American navy, was a Kirkcudbrightshire man.

As Nelson was manoeuvring before Trafalgar, a number of Scots tars were watching the scene. Nelson hoisted his famous signal "England expects. . . ."

One of the Scots began to grumble, "England, ye see, aye England. No a word o' Scotland though there are hunners o' oor folk here the-day, forbye Nelson's ain doctor, Beattie, a Dumfriesshire man."

"Haud your tongue, man," grunted another old salt, "Div ye no think that Nelson kens fine whit he's daein'. He kens it wad be a fair affront to remind a Scotsman that he's expectit to dae his duty."

The same spirit was manifested when a number of Scots were in a crowded London pub after being evacuated from Dunkirk.

"Man, Geordie," confided one in a stage whisper, which was clearly audible all through the pub, "This is goin' to be a hell o' a long war."

Everyone looked up, and indignant protests came from all quarters, but the speaker had not finished.

"Aye, it's goin' to be a hell o' a lang war, especially if England capitulates." (Uproar.)

There was a popular song about, at that time, which was never off the radio,
    "There'll always be an England
    And England shall be free."
Many near riots were caused by parodies of this song. One of them went something like this,
    "There'll always be an England
    And England shall be free
    So long as there's a Scotsman left
    In the good old K.O.S.B. (King's Own Scottish Borderers.)
Some were so much more provocative that I refrain from quoting them.

A year or two ago I would have been run in by the Dutch police if I had been able to find a half-brick to pitch through the plate-glass window of the British European Airways office in the Central Station, Rotterdam.

In the window was a large-sized coloured poster of a piper with Edinburgh Castle in the background, entitled Edinburgh, England. I tried to get a copy to display in Edinburgh, but understandably none was available for export. It is no excuse to say the Rotterdammers think Scotland is a part of England, for I have attended the Scottish Church quite close to the Central Station. It was rebuilt after the old Scots Kirk was destroyed by Hitler in 1940, when he bombed the centre of the city.

The language problem always remains a barrier, however one tries to remove it. After the Union the Scots members were subject to ridicule in Parliament when they rose to speak as no doubt the English members would have been had Parliament been assembled in Edinburgh. The Scots decided on a compromise (which sounds more like a surrender.) They began to learn English.

David Hume, the historian and philosopher undertook to teach the English idiom to his countrymen, and made a list of Scotticisms to be avoided. Dr Johnson found this amusing, and commented, "I wonder that *he* should find them." Hume's first "History" had been full of Scotticisms.

Sir John Sinclair, the publisher of the First Statistical Account of Scotland, also set to work with other writers to Anglicise his countrymen with a volume of Scotticisms to be put right.

But all these efforts have had very little effect for the Scots still stick to their own form of speech. In any case it is of little use trying to acquire a new language to disguise one's mother tongue. It never deceives anyone for long.

An elderly Scotsman who had lived in Paris for several years was well-known to have a great contempt for everything that was not connected with Scotland.

A young Englishman who had lived in Perthshire for many years and had acquired a fair knowledge of Scots, thought he would cheer up the old man by visiting him and talking about his native land.

But his kindness was ill-rewarded, for the Scot, after a time, began to suspect a certain falseness in his visitor's accents. He dismissed him rudely, "Ach, awa' wi ye. Ye're nae Scotsman after a'. You're just an improved Englishman."

A servant lassie returned for a holiday from a year or two in London. She was asked how she got on with the language problem. Had she continued to use Scots?

"O, no, they wad never hae kent whit I was at. I had to learn the English."

"Hoo did ye manage that? It maun hae been gey hard."

"Ach, no, it was gey easy. I just missed oot a' the Rs and gaed the words a bit chow in the middle."

Great cities have their local dialects which are unintelligible a few miles away. Paris has its peculiar slang; so have Amsterdam, London and Glasgow. In many cases it is a corrupt form of the national language. The rhyming slang of the Cockney where sisters are toe-blisters, is just as puzzling as Glaswegian where after a minor street accident this conversation was heard.

"Whasamarra?"

"A fellafellaffalorra."

"Was rafellaon a lorra when rafellafellaff?"

In the 1914-18 war an English Guards regiment was resting by the roadside when a few companies of Glasgow 'Banties' marched past. They were men a few inches below the acceptable army stature, but this was no reflection on their toughness and their fighting qualities.

As they marched past the Guards, they were subjected to a lot of cross-fire.

"Does your mother know you're out?" quizzed a tall Cockney guardsman.

A dour wee five-foot-nothing replied to the taunt, over his shoulder, with a bit of repartee in the lilt of the "Toonheid."

"Aye, fine that, sonny, and when ye gae hame tell your mither ye've seen the sodgers."

The same wild-fowl from the jungles of Polmadie, where once the marshes bred coot, duck and water-hens, before the city spread its suburbs, were engaged in clearing a ditch in the very rainy Flemish autumn of 1917. A brass-hat and his staff drew up in a car and surveyed the company of mud-drenched banties. Addressing no-one in particular the lordly one asked, "What regiment is this?"

"The **Bantams**, sir," answered an N.C.O.

"Ah, the Bantams, how very interesting," he drawled, fixing the very angry sodden Glaswegians with his monocle. This was more than flesh and blood could stand.

An angry wee fella shouted, "Aye, whae the bloody hell did ye think we was? A flock o' fuckin' water-hens?"

A Scot in England was recalling a nightmare he had had, and the crowded hotel-bar was listening.

"I dreamt I was in Hell. It was fair awfu' what wi' the noise and the smell and the crowds."

"Full of Scotsmen, I suppose, paying at last for their pleasures," quipped an Englishman.

"O, aye, I saw mony o' my auld acquaintances. Then a chiel I thocht I recognised came up and spoke.

"Hoo are ye John? I'm Auld Nick. Would ye like a conducted tour o' the regions?"

So off a party o' us set and were shown intae a' the rooms. There were some fu' o' Frenchies, some o' Irish, Danes, a' bleezin awa and howlin' blue murder. Then we opened a door and were nearly chokit wi' sic a rush o' thick reek.

'Wha's in there?' I askit Auld Nick.

'O. that's a big room fu' o' Englishmen. They're ower green to burn.' "

Here is a tale of Feb. 7, 1787.

A citizen of Edinburgh burst into the house of a neighbour, his eyes filled with tears of mingled sorrow and anger. His friends had never seen him in such a state; they asked if he had had bad news or had suffered a domestic loss. Finally he managed to gasp out:

"It cam on me a' o' a sudden, as I was suppin' my parritch, that it is twa hunner years to the vera day since oor bonnie Queen Mary was beheidit by that thrawn bitch, Queen Elizabeth o' England, while yon thowless sumph Jamie Sax ne'er fashed his thoomb aboot his puir mither that brocht him intae this weary warld."

The heather was on fire; the lion was rampant that February day in 1587.

All Scotland, Hielands and Lawlands, was roused to fiercest anger and preparations were set agoing to march for vengeance. King James managed, for his own ends, to calm things down.

But Scotland, and the world, has never forgotten.

One of the most famous philosophers of all time was Duns Scotus, who was born near Duns, in Berwickshire seven centuries ago. He did not appreciate any gibes directed at his native land.

He was a great wit as well as a subtle philosopher. At the court of Charles of Burgundy, as the two faced one another at dinner, the Duke rather boorishly asked him "What is the difference between a sot and a Scot?" (In Old French the play on words was possible.) The theologian answered "There is only a table between them." (a table meaning also a thin sheet of parchment). Charles' character was well-known and there was a roar at his discomfiture.

The scholarly reputation of Duns Scotus is renowned all over the world; there are Scots who have none of his ability, but a much larger share of ambition, which makes them ridiculous.

The S.N.P. candidate for Argyll visited the island of Gigha to canvas for votes, and was met by a gentleman who claimed to be the Prime minister of Gigha. When asked if he supported the Scottish National Party's claim for independence, he replied in the affirmative, on condition that once Scotland gained independence, the island of Gigha would be given independence, as they had a tremendous ambition to achieve. The candidate asked what this might be but was refused any further information. However, he was offered the hospitality of the Prime minister's house that evening, and after a few drams the Prime minister said "Ye seem a ferry nice chap. I'll tell you our ambition; it's to rule the World."

Sassenach was a Gaelic word for Saxons and to the Highlanders it meant anyone on the East coast of Scotland who was not a Gael. There was a sound reason for this, because Lothian was an Anglian province, and most of the central lowlands were populated by people of Germanic stock. During the Norman oppressions too, Saxons by the thousands fled to Scotland, as a welcoming country.

In Ayton's "Burial March of Dundee" we have these lines from the battle of Killiecrankie, where Highlanders were opposed by Lowlanders, "Leslie's foot and Leven's troopers," supported by Dutch soldiers.

> Then we bounded from our covert,
> Judge how looked the *Saxons* then
> When they saw the rugged mountain
> Start to life with armed men."

To apply the term Sassenach to all Englishmen is clearly wrong. In many areas of England, particularly in the West Country, the population is of Celtic strain, descended from the original British tribes, as also are the Welsh; and according to reliable ethnologists, regions such as Allendale in Northumberland, and the Forest of Arden, in Shakespeare's Warwickshire, are predominantly Celtic.

The prickliness shown by the Scots towards England is not directed at the English people, but at the political establishment and the attitude it encourages to treat Scots as a race outside the Pale. The stories I have told are simply Scotland's small compensation for the major neglect or worse they have suffered for so long.

GLOSSARY

BAIRNS
dook—dip
dub—puddle
gimmer—young ewe
guider—child's cart
kyte—stomach
lanesome—lonesome
shilpet—slim
skelpit—smacked
steched—full
thon—that

LOVE
ava—at all
brant—had the boar
brods—boards
chappit—struck
claes—clothes
cowp-cairt—large trouser fly
cowpt—upset
fashin—troubling
glaikt—cheated
grice—piglet
ham cloots—open drawers
hure—whore
lowp—leap
lowsed—loosened
muckle-moo'ed—big-mouthed
neist—next
nock—clock
rig-bane—backbone
set tae—set to
steek—stitch
stour—dust
swallies—swallows
swatches—cloth cuttings
sweir—unwilling
tattie—potato
wheecht—whipped off

MEAT AND MUSIC
buik—bulk
byre—cow-shed
coo-platt—cow's dropping
dreepin'—dripping
kist o' whistles—an organ
lave—remainder
lug o' a haddie—haddock belly
neeps—turnips

neive—fist
rizzert—dried
steikit—clenched
smoorit—smothered
thole—endure
waucht—big drink

DRINK
bedirten—dirty
cleckin—litter
cloot—cloth
dreept—dripped
gars—makes, forces
guid—good
happit—wrapped
pap o' ma hass—uvula
soom—swim
wheen—quantity

SPORT
Ailsa chuckers—Ailsa Craig stones
bauchles—old shoes
bonspiel—a large curling match
Carron airn—Carron iron
chiel—man
dormie—unbeatable
dozin—spinning
"Draps o' Brandy"—a dance
fell—very
gowff—golf
gutty ba'—gutta percha golf ball
imphm—yes
keek—peep
peerie—spinning top
pliskies—tricks
pooch—pocket
quat—quit
reid Carsphairn—red Carsphairn granite
rinks—teams
skraigh—streak
stell—enclosure
yuckers—boulders

BEASTS
aith—oath
bandy—bent
bawbee—halfpenny
birse—bristle
bubbly-jock—turkey-cock

139

bykes—wasps' or bees' nests
caller—fresh
dairy deemies—dairy maids
flyped—turned inside out
hairst—harvest
hauden doon—imposed upon
laigh—low
loonie—boy
nicky tams—ploughman's garters
soo—sow
waddin'—wedding
weskit—waistcoat

THE KIRK

chappit—struck
chuckie-stane—pebble
ding—strike
dozened—quietened
fash—concern
gousty—capacious
greet—weep
joukit—dodged
lugs—ears
nebs—noses, beaks
roupy—hoarse
scunner—dislike
skailing—spilling, emptying
taen up wi'—attracted to
threty—thirty
unco—very
yerkit—jerked

AULD NICK

beckit—curtseyed
bourtrees—elder trees
channerin'—fretting
gamfled—flirted
gaislins—goslings
houghmagandie—fornication
kent—bludgeon
kittle cattle—untrustworthy
leugh—laugh
libbet—castrated
lowe—flame
maun—must
ride the stang—ride the rail
scouther—roast
stappit—stuffed

THE HEREAFTER

attacked—approached to talk
ding—strike
dockan—dock plant
flaff—flash
gilpy—young girl
girnin'—grimacing
tedding—ricking

POETS

cauld—cold
clarty—dirty
crowdie—brose
dowp—bottom
farrow—give birth to piglets
gerss—grass
howdie—midwife
kirned—churned
lear—learning
mim—silent
neives—fists
sharny—dungy
sturt—surprise
wame—belly

FOOLS AND FOLLIES

bree—broth
clappit een on—seen
cuddy—horse
cuit—heel
dug's hass—dog's throat
feel—fool
gliff—glance
guff—stench
kittley—itchy
pudden—pudding
theikin—thatching
whang—slice
wyce—sensible

THE PRACTICAL SCOT

chaft—jaw
daud—blow, slap
deiving—deafening
dirl—rattle
dunt—heavy blow
gadie—light-headed
griddle—girdle

140

kye—cows
plump—dip
wallop—stir
warsling—wrestling

THE GREAT DIVIDE

beets—boots
breed Skwytland—broad Scotland
freaks—tricks
gloamin—twilight
gweed—good
humphy back—hunchback
jabberin—chattering

kyloes—cattle
lift—sky
plaister—label
reived—stole
sheen—shoes
wap—stroke

THE THISTLE

chow—chew
rowed—rolled
sumph—idiot
thowless—useless
thrawn—ill-tempered